THE **CALL** TO

Life Stories

Craig Winston LeCroy
Arizona State University

Sage Publications
International Educational and Professional Publisher
Thousand Oaks ▪ London ▪ New Delhi

For information:

Sage Publications, Inc.
2455 Teller Road
Thousand Oaks, California 91320
E-mail: order@sagepub.com

Sage Publications Ltd.
6 Bonhill Street
London EC2A 4PU
United Kingdom

Sage Publications India Pvt. Ltd.
M-32 Market
Greater Kailash I
New Delhi 110 048 India

Printed in the United States of America

Library of Congress Cataloging-in-Publication Data

LeCroy, Craig W.
   The call to social work: Life stories/by Craig Winston LeCroy.
      p.cm.
   ISBN 0-7619-8568-9 (p)
   1. Social service. 2. Social workers. I. Title.
   HV40 .L38 2002
   361.3--dc21
                        20021007179

Acquiring Editor:	Steven Rutter
Production Editor:	Denise Santoyo
Typesetter:	Siva Math Setters, Chennai, India
Cover Designer:	Michelle Lee

For all social workers
who have important stories to tell

Contents

Acknowledgments

First and foremost, I am grateful to the many social workers who consented to be interviewed, shared their real-life stories, spoke earnestly about what they do, and allowed me to record their histories. Documenting the life histories of social workers will lead to a better understanding of social work and the experience of being a social worker. I worked on this book over a period of many years, and many people made important contributions to the final product. More than any other writing I have published, this book is the combination of many people's combined efforts. I received support and assistance in interviewing participants by Lori Chang, Shawnee Inez, and Lyndi Rivers. Linda Ramirez was essential to the project, providing all of the transcription. Allyson LaBrue provided valuable word-processing support and editorial assistance. Several people provided critical assistance in editing the hundreds of pages of transcription that became the final product: Mike Mulcahy, Jan Daley, Jeannine Chapelle, and especially Ellen McFall and Kathy Lortie. Ellen and Kathy worked closely with me in reshaping the stories and assisted me in cutting down the material when I could not bear to see even a sentence cut from the final interviews. Steven Rutter, president of Pine Forge Press, provided ongoing confidence, encouragement, and support in this project. Although there are many more social workers, many more fields of practice, and many more target groups of clients and difficulties that could be represented in this book, I believe this sample of social workers provides a glimpse into the heart and soul of social work.

For additional information, updates, discussion questions,
or to schedule presentations about *The Call to Social Work*,
visit my website at:
http://www.public.asu.edu/~lecroy/thecalltosocialwork

Prologue

The idea to write this book came from my work as a professor at the university. Every fall, as the tormenting heat of summer loosens its grip, students show up to embark on a calling—a calling to become professional social workers. I am privileged to help nurture their calling as they learn about the practice of social work in my class, Social Work 510. I begin that class by enlarging students' notions about social work practice. We talk about what social work is, who does it, and how it is done. Social work is indeed a diverse profession—difficult for one person to describe with limited experience. So every year, I invite different social workers to a panel discussion about the work they do. I usually have about four or five social workers on the panel. The students and I pummel them with questions about their lives as social workers: Why did you decide to do social work? What do you like the most and least about your work? Don't you get depressed after seeing all those abused children? What does being a professional social worker mean to you personally? As we listen to the social workers respond to these questions, the special calling of being a social worker emerges.

Every fall, when the panel discussion concludes, I leave the class respectful of and reflective about these people, these social workers who work hard to provide special help to others. I believe it is, as Gregg Levoy describes, a calling—a meaningful and authentic life that these people have found and are following.[1] Sherrie Connelly refers to the development of "work spirit," the spark and vitality people express when they love what they do.[2] When my students sit down in those

1

hard, small desk chairs to begin their first class, they are responding to a calling deep within themselves, a desire to leave behind the banal day-to-day struggle and enter a world with greater meaning, develop an expanded social consciousness, and strengthen connections to fellow humankind. Maslow talks about the innate desire people have to "actualize" themselves and pursue "peak experiences" after their basic needs are met.[3] For many people, being a social worker is a pathway to better know life, discover its meaning, and obtain a higher sense of connection with the world.

This book is titled *The Call to Social Work* because I believe many people are called to do social work. Their efforts are to contribute to compassion and justice in the world, to pursue social transformations, to provide a vision for a better way of living. Their day-to-day work is encircled by compassionate treatment of others. Because of their calling most of them have immense hearts and deep souls.

What can we learn by listening to the stories about the work of the social worker? We can learn about people who are drawn to help others, people who are committed to pursuing their visions of a better world. Work, as Matthew Fox tells us, "comes from inside out; work is the expression of our soul, our inner being."[4] Many people are "worked" instead of working. Social workers choose their work, often after dissatisfaction with a previous job. This allows them the opportunity to heed Aquinas's words, "to live well is to work well, or display a good activity."[5] Social work is, for many, a pathway to transformative work- for themselves, others, and the community. As such, much can be learned from understanding the life and work of the social worker.

❖ LIFE STORIES: A COLLECTION OF WISDOM

As Rachel Naomi Remen reminds us, "everybody is a story."[6] Stories contain important grains of wisdom, and together, they can build castles of knowledge about the world. We are rediscovering the importance of stories. Without stories, we lose important wisdom about who we are. There is indeed value in "kitchen table wisdom," as we pass stories along to each other. Remen invites us to take a seat at life's kitchen table. This book is about a kitchen table that is surrounded by social workers, all telling stories about their lives. And although we have much information about how to be a professional social worker, what about how to live as a social worker? What can we learn from this perspective?

As social workers describe their life stories and the life stories of others, we learn about the mysteries of life. And although many of the social workers' clients have painful and sad stories, they are stories about life lessons. They provide a perspective that puts one's own life into a unique frame of reference. Listening to stories can be healing.

A deep trust of life often emerges when you listen to other people's stories. "You realize you're not alone; you're traveling in wonderful company. Ordinary people living ordinary lives often are heros," says Remen.[7]

Carol Bly argues that the power in a story is the "experience of the other."[8] Have you ever wondered what a social worker does? What it is like to be a social worker? Who are these merchants of morality that commit their lives to solving the ills of society, who peer into the darkest human basement? Social workers know and understand the depths of the human experience. They are present when abused children are removed from parents, when husbands batter their wives, when 12-year-old girls report they are pregnant.

❖ THE SOCIAL WORK PROFESSION AND CONTEMPORARY SOCIAL WORK PRACTICE

Although the work in this book is not composed of a representative sample of social work, it does allow one to see the hearts and souls of social workers—social workers who have not abandoned their mission. They wake up every day to new challenges in helping people struggle to put food on the table, get needed medical and social services, follow through on commitments to quit drugs, and face death with dignity. They are committed to the ideals of social work, hard working, underpaid, and earnest in their attempts to make this a better place for the people with whom they work. Social work and society have a lot to learn about this world by listening to the voices of contemporary social workers. Most books attribute much to the pioneers of social work; my book is dedicated to contemporary social workers.

My efforts in interviewing social workers about their work were an attempt to build a stronger bridge between the sterile academic discourse about social work and the day-to-day practice of social work.

The social work profession is filled with books that describe social work and its building blocks. Here is a foundation made of concrete; this is a 2" x 4", and after you construct a wooden frame, you nail sheet rock on to it. You can describe all of these building materials, or you can show someone what it is like to build a house and talk with them about their experience. What is it like to drive nails into two-by-fours all day long? How does it feel to start with a foundation and end up with a completely built house? My quest was to bring to readers more information about the everyday practice of social work. At the end of a day, what kind of self-doubts, humility, and self-reflections are on the mind of a social worker? I wanted a window into the life of a social worker. So I talked with social workers, recorded and transcribed what was said, read and reviewed the interviews, and edited and refashioned them until their stories became the ink on these pages.

In many ways, our textbooks about social work take what is real about everyday practice and turn it into textual constructions about the social work profession.[9] This makes sense for the design of a textbook, but it does not help anyone who wants to look through the eyes and breathe the air of a social worker. Siporin's definition that "social workers are professional helpers designated by society to aid people who are distressed, disadvantaged, disabled, defeated, or dependent" does not help you know what it is like to *do* social work.[10]

A critical question for the profession is, What do social workers do? This question is how many textbooks in the field start. It was also a guiding question when a group of social work educators and practitioners met with the National Association of Social Workers to explore developments within the social work profession. Social work is described in various ways—the unloved profession, a profession of many faces, the caring profession—but rarely has it been described by social workers themselves. From a textbook point of view, to understand social work is to "appreciate the contributions of Jane Addams and Mary Richmond to the social change and individual service missions of social work."[11] Every textbook on social work I could find harkens back to the seminal contributions of these two women. And I have no doubt about their importance. But where is the understanding of contemporary social work? Jane Addams and Mary Richmond never even thought of people who suffer from HIV, wouldn't recognize wife battering, had no notion of the problems of urban homelessness. The question of what social workers do cannot be fully answered without narrative descriptions from contemporary social workers.

Social work has evolved, and to truly understand this evolution, we need to understand more intimately what social workers do. There is another world of social work, a world that is filled with mystery, intimate encounters with clients, spiritual awakenings, the everyday grind of work, and a long view about how being a social worker makes sense in the 21st century. There have been shockingly few attempts to capture this day-to-day reality of social work. If we had good narrative descriptions of practice over time, we could investigate how the daily practice of social work has evolved.

❖ BUILDING LIFE STORIES: THE RESEARCH INTERVIEW AS CONVERSATION

The method of gathering the information for this book is based on qualitative research interviewing. Kvale aptly describes a traveler metaphor to illustrate research interviewing.[12] In this metaphor, the interviewer is a traveler on a journey that leads to a story told on returning home. The interviewer-traveler explores new landscapes by having conversations with the people along the way. The traveler may seek to find certain places by following a method—a path that leads to a goal. "The interviewer wanders along with the local inhabitants, asks questions that lead the subjects to tell their own stories of their lived world, and converses with them in the original Latin meaning of conversation as 'wandering together with.'"[13]

In this approach, the researcher or reporter listens to what is described qualitatively and reconstructs stories about what is learned. Meaning is brought to light in the interviews by the researcher's interpretations, and stories or tales are "remolded into new narratives."[14] The interviews or conversations can create new understanding. This notion of conversation as research is defined as "an interview whose purpose is to obtain descriptions of the world of the interviewee with respect to interpreting the meaning of the described phenomena."[15] This view is similar to the oral history method of Studs Terkel.[16] Terkel is well respected as a great conversationalist. Although his methods are more from the journalist side of things, he was able to bring forth stories from people and then retell the critical parts. Like the oral history method of Terkel, the interviews for this book all begin with a few set questions, but ultimately, the conversations follow the storytellers' lead—building on what seems to matter the most to the person. All interviews were tape recorded and transcribed. The transcriptions were then edited into narrative life stories. With only a few exceptions, all persons in this book are identified by their real names.

The interviews were conducted in a manner that addressed the following aspects of qualitative research: *Life world*, to enter and understand the everyday lived world of the social worker and his or her relation to it; *Meaning*, to understand and interpret the meaning of central themes in the life world of the social worker; *Specificity*, to obtain descriptions of specific situations; *Focus*, to focus the interview on themes as they emerge; *Qualitative knowledge*, to obtain qualitative knowledge as expressed by social workers; and *Deliberate näiveté*, to be open to any new and unexpected phenomena.[17]

The social workers in this book were selected on a nonrandom basis. I used a snowball sampling approach, asking people I knew to give me names of social workers to contact for interviewing. I wanted social workers who were doing the day-to-day activities of "social work." In general, I attempted to select a wide variety of social workers—differing in age, geographic location, and racial and social background. I decided to not identify individuals but to let the story represent their own self-descriptions. Hence, some voices are people of color but remain color blind; some voices are of BSWs and some are of MSWs; some voices are old and some are young.

Each life story in this book represents a true picture of what the social worker said. Although some book reviewers suggested I edit out aspects of the person's voice that did not portray social work positively or that represented a questionable aspect of social work practice, I was not interested in such portrayals. The purpose of this book is to accurately capture the thought and deeds of social workers—the good and bad. Instructors who use this book in their courses will have to contrast their ideals of practice with the realities captured in each life story. Students who read this book will have to think about whether each story represents good practice or what principles they would adhere to based on their understanding of social work. But in a book attempting a modern description of social work practice, this is how it should be because the common denominator is the reality of doing social work.

The Call to Social Work is a presentation of narrative descriptions about the work and life of contemporary social workers. If you are reading this book because you are interested in social work as a career, you will gain a perspective from these stories that cannot be obtained from textbooks about social work. You will develop an understanding of what social workers do and learn, about what they think and feel, and about what they do. If you are a practicing social worker, reading *The Call to Social Work* will help you place your work in a broader context. When you ask yourself at the end of a day, "What have I really done?" and are searching for greater meaning, it is helpful to share in the wisdom of others, to sit at the kitchen table where people have similar stories to tell.

And if you are not a social worker and are not interested in social work as a career, *The Call to Social Work* can teach you about life. What is it like to pursue ideals of compassion and justice? How do social workers face the day-to-day pressures of children burned and beaten by their parents, children abandoned and unloved, adults struggling with demons and hallucinations that torture them, and people who must cope with the everyday tragedies of life—loss of loved ones from automobile accidents, the pain of infertility, the struggle of helping children with behavior disorders, and coping with increasing hearing loss? With the tragedies come the blessings: helping an adult find and keep a job for the first time, getting adolescents to accept that suicide is not their best option, facilitating the adoption of a child with new parents, helping immigrants adapt to a new society, providing new services to those who need them, and building new communities of hope. Social work is indeed about life itself.

❖ **NOTES**

1. Gregg Levoy, *Callings: Finding and Following an Authentic Life* (New York: Harmony Books, 1997).
2. Sherrie Connelly, "Work Spirit," *The Family Therapy Networker* (March/April, 1996): 11.
3. Abraham Maslow, *Toward a Psychology of Being* (Van Nostrand Reinhold, 1968).
4. Matthew Fox, *The Reinvention of Work: A New Vision of Livelihood for Our Time* (HarperSanFrancisco, 1994), 5.

5. Matthew Fox, *Sheer Joy: Conversations With Thomas Aquinas on Creation Spirituality* (San Francisco: Harper San Francisco, 1992), 186.
6. Rachel Naomi Remen, *Kitchen Table Wisdom* (New York: Riverhead Books, 1996).
7. Remen, *Kitchen Table Wisdom*, p. xvii.
8. Carol Bly, "Stories," *Utne Reader* (July/August 1997): 22.
9. Gerald A.J. de Montigny, *Social Working: An Ethnography of Front-Line Practice* (Toronto: University of Toronto Press, 1995).
10. Max Siporin, *Introduction to Social Work Practice* (New York: Macmillan Publishing, 1975).
11. Armando Morales and Bradford Sheafor, *Social Work: A Profession of Many Faces* (Boston: Allyn and Bacon, 1998), xvi.
12. Steinar Kvale, *InterViews: An Introduction to Qualitative Research Interviewing* (Thousand Oaks, CA: Sage, 1996).
13. Kvale, *InterViews*, p. 4.
14. Kvale, *InterViews*, p. 4.
15. Kvale, *InterViews*, p. 6
16. See Studs Terkel, *Working: People Talk About What They Do All Day and How They Feel About What They Do* (New York: Ballantine Books, 1972).
17. Kvale, *InterViews*, p. 30-31.

1

The Art of Doing Social Work

❖ **ELIZABETH DAY**

When I was 7, I saw a March of Dimes ad on TV, and it was a little boy sitting in a wheelchair with adults standing next to him. I yelled to my mother, "Come here and look at the TV. What is it called when a person helps another person?" She said, "A social worker." Now, if she had said a counselor or a physical therapist, I would have decided to be that, but from that day on, whenever anyone asked me what I wanted to be when I grew up, it was a social worker.

We lived in South Africa when I was a child. It was in the late '50s, and most Americans didn't even know that Apartheid existed. When I lived in South Africa, all white kids under age 9 had a black nanny. You did everything with your nanny. In public, there were four bathrooms: one for black men, one for white men, one for white women, and one for black women. Until age 9, you went in the bathroom for black women with your nanny. I went into one of these bathrooms early on, and it was so horrible that I just decided I would never go to any public bathroom when I was out with my nanny.

In comparison to other white South African families, our family had a very different feeling about our nanny, Eunice. We loved Eunice and felt that she was a family member. I had long conversations with Eunice about what life was like for her growing up. Her description of her life was similar to living in this country on an Indian reservation, where a certain tribe would have a portion of land, and that was primarily where they would live. She would ride the bus in from town to where we lived. She would stay and work during the week and then go back home on the weekends.

Living in that system was very difficult for me. I had a lot of discussions with Eunice trying to get it straight in my mind. I cried myself to sleep most nights just wondering how human beings could have such a skewed view of each other. I would go to church and hear that God is love and God created people equally, and I would say, "Excuse me. Why are there only white children in the Sunday school?" The Sunday school teachers just didn't know what to say because they had been brought up from the time they could walk to feel that people who had darker skin were lesser in some way. I would say, "That is not what it says here in the Bible, and that is not what you are teaching me. Why are you saying that?" It was incongruent, and the adults could see that when they were sitting there talking with a child, but it was such a persuasive thought in the society that stepping beyond it was very hard.

My experiences in South Africa cemented my interest in trying to see all people as special and important. No matter how bleak the situation looks, everyone deserves to be loved, to be respected, and to be given the opportunity to shine in their own way.

Another experience that influenced me was my time as a high school exchange student in Bolivia. I lived in a town about 3 hours outside of La Paz, which is the capital of Bolivia. It was 13,000 feet above sea level. It was a mining town, and a large portion of the people in and around the city lived in abject poverty. I mean poverty that we, in America, can't even imagine. During that winter when I went to school, I wore two pairs of socks, a pair of nylons, football socks that came up to my knees, wool pants, a long wool mini coat, a hat with a hood, a scarf wrapped around me, and gloves. I wore all of these clothes all day because the school wasn't heated. Yet wearing all that, I walked to school passing women and children who were sitting out on the street wearing cotton shirts and cotton skirts and sandals made out of old tires. That was a pivotal experience in terms of seeing that the world is truly not a fair place and that there are people hurting more than you can put into words.

I work in the school system now, and it seems that problems in our society are getting more and more complex. Children are dealing with much more at a younger age. Life has become frantic. Maybe the pioneer children had to deal with things that were just as bad, but they were different kinds of things. I like my work in the school setting because there are a lot of professionals working toward the same goal of supporting families and children.

One thing that I did as a school social worker was evaluate students to see if they qualified for special education. The social worker's role was to interview the parent, be an advocate, and get information. A child is like a puzzle, with different professions looking at different pieces. The psychologist is looking at the intelligence and natural capability of the child. The teacher is looking at how that child interacts with other children and how he learns on a day-to-day basis. And the special education social worker is responsible for helping the parents bring their pieces of the puzzle to the table. I think we often forget how important that parent piece is. I enjoyed that role a great deal. I was able to talk with parents about the developmental history of the child, the child's strengths, and the areas where there were problems. A lot of times, what I heard from the parent during the home visit was different than what I heard at the school.

As a school social worker, one of the first groups that I ran at a middle school was a grief group. We had eight or nine kids that had parents who had been murdered or who had died in some tragic way. We did different activities and things that you would expect to do in a grief group. Some weeks, I thought that those things worked really well, and some weeks I thought they didn't. There was one student who didn't say a whole lot. It seemed right not to push her, and she kept coming, so we kept including her. The very last session of our group, towards the end, out of the blue, she said, "I've brought something to show you all." She pulled out a picture of her mother who had been murdered in a very horrible way. There was dead silence for a minute, and we all caught our breath. We really cared about her. Unfortunately, because her life was in such a shambles, there wasn't a whole lot I could do. I could have worked with that kid from now until the cows came home, but there were just too many things going on in her life that were impossible to fix. But we looked at that picture of her mother and let her know we cared. She can carry that in her heart forever. And maybe knowing that someone cared about her at that one point in her life helped her later on. Maybe she has no recollection of that group experience whatsoever. We did the best we could, and I hope we helped her.

About 4 years ago, I switched from being a regular school social worker to coordinating the Family Resource and Wellness Center. I made that move because I like the collaborative aspect of the Wellness Center. I'm a firm believer in working as a team. I see that there are a lot of families that could be utilizing services, moving forward, and doing wonderful things, but there are so many barriers in their way. The idea of the Family Resource and Wellness Center is to try to go past those barriers and make bridges for people to get the services they need.

A barrier that seems very tiny to us could be huge to another person. For instance, one of the first years we were open, a mom came in who hadn't had heating in her home for 2 years. She had a couple of kids, and one of them had asthma. We were able to find an organization that would fix her heating for free. I thought this problem was going to be a cinch to solve. She didn't have a phone, so we told her to come in and use our phone to arrange a time for her heater to be serviced. She was real excited, and she came in and made the phone call and then hung up and started walking out of the room. We asked her what happened, and she said that there was an answering machine, and she couldn't leave a message on an answering machine. We said, "Time out. Sit down, and we will show you how to leave your name. You will be nervous, but we can practice until you are comfortable." So we practiced a couple of times, and she called again and left her name on the answering machine. They got in contact with her, and a couple of days later, she had heat. Here was a woman who was literally willing to forgo getting heat in her house because she couldn't leave a message on the answering machine. It is a perfect example of a barrier that to you or me would be no big deal.

One of the first things that you need to know as a social worker is that you have to separate yourself from your work. You can't take everything home. As you grow as a social worker, you develop the ability to separate yourself from the horrible things that you hear and see. At the end of the day, you need to go home and be a part of your family. You don't have to lose your sense of compassion and genuine caring, but you do have to make some separation.

I have been reading about how the clergy are having more problems in their personal lives with things like divorce, alcoholism, et cetera. I think social workers are probably in the same camp; we just haven't read about them recently because no one has done a study focusing on social workers. It is difficult to see all the hurt and then shift your focus to completing your monthly report so the program can continue. We all deal with those frustrations. What really carries me from one place to the next are those little triumphs, and sometimes they are very little. I have to keep moving on. Some days, you have to just take a deep breath and do it. You've heard the old adage, "Fake it until you make it." Sometimes, you just can't do any more than that. I've been in social work for most of my life, and I'll always be a social worker in my heart.

❖ CATHY SAMMONS

Working with disabled children has been the pivotal experience in my whole life and career. I became totally enamored of people with mental retardation, autism, and cerebral palsy. What I grew to love was not so much the direct work with children but the work with parents. I was exposed to the hardest thing that I ever had to do in my career then—and it is still the hardest thing I have to do—which is to tell parents that their child has a developmental disability.

I would look into the eyes of a parent, and while I was telling them this terrible news and though my heart was heavy with sadness, *I* wanted to be the one to tell them. I didn't want some insensitive technician telling them this news. I had seen it done poorly a lot. I'd seen people told devastating things in hallways, and professionals who were so inept that even when they thought they were being sensitive, they would say things like, "I know you are feeling a lot of guilt right now," just leaping to conclusions that were unfounded and patronizing.

I have this profound identification with parents who are going through this. Some of it was because so many of the disciplines were critical of parents. They would give them instructions and tell them to do this or that: tell them what kind of diet the child should be on, with X number of calories, or this vitamin, or how they should be brushing their child's teeth. These children can be difficult to manage, and professionals threw parents all these expectations. When they didn't do them just perfectly, they were judged. I saw the parents as being alone while hearing this advice, which is all good advice, but nobody was helping them turn the advice into a daily reality. To me, that was the most exciting and intellectually challenging and emotionally important part of the whole thing. You get nine disciplines telling you what to do, but only the 10th one, social work, is going to help you do it. Only social work will help you to decide if you *wanted* to do all those nine things, and if you did, what did you want to do first, and what did you want to do last. And only social work will help you look at the fact that some of those things might interfere with your marriage or interfere with the care of the siblings—or maybe violate your cultural values.

I was learning that the distinction between social work and the other fields was that the other fields were technicians, and they were committed to *fixing* things, but social workers weren't about fixing things. That has challenged me in my career because sometimes you meet clients who expect you to be a technician and look at you as a fixer. But other clients realize that what they are hungering for is the person who is not going to be the fixer and not going to be the prescriber but will help them put everything together, process it, make decisions, and take action.

I committed myself to developmental disabilities, and my first job was working with families in a rural area. I got to do home visits. That was a peak experience because all my training was in the office and in a hospital. Visiting families in their homes was such a gift and so incredible. I was service coordinator for 30 to 50 families, and I learned so much from them.

I had one family in the newborn intensive care unit, a teen couple who had given birth to a baby who was encephalic, which is a condition where the brain has not developed. They wanted to take the baby home, but the hospital didn't want them to. The baby was going to die and needed to be held and tube fed. I was working with the team to allow this couple to take the baby home to die. It was a moving and profound experience for me. The teenage mother said, "This is my baby, and I want to get him home like any other mother takes her baby home. I know this is going to happen, and you're telling me it will happen, and it's hopeless. OK. But at least I can take him home. I have a bassinet for him, I have clothes, and I can feed him." The issue was, could she be trusted with the tube feeding? Would she learn that? The answer was that we would give it a try because that was the healing and empowering path for the family.

A social worker has to wear three hats, which no other professional wears in combination. The first one is that of teacher, because information is important and because information can set you free. Information can empower. In the medical world, so much of the time, the patient is walled off from information. They are protected from it in this paternalistic approach: "There are some things that the patient doesn't need to know, can't know, shouldn't know, isn't ready to know." I don't buy any of that; I think you need access to information and facilitation to understand it. The social worker can be the best teacher.

But information is not the whole story. The second hat is that of a therapist, someone who can relay the *meaning* of the information that is most profound for the individual. It is not the facts that they are told but what those facts mean and how the individual interprets them. For instance, I became a specialist in genetic counseling, and I did my master's thesis on the emotional impact of prenatal genetic screening. It was a wonderful example of the way that information can be processed differently depending on your personality, culture, and life experience. You can say to one family that their risk of having a child with X condition is 90% or 95%, and one family would say, "Oh, what a relief. We have a chance to have a child who is healthy." The next family would say, "Oh, alright. We need to terminate the pregnancy. With odds like that, we'd be crazy to go through with this pregnancy." You learn that even though they both have exactly the same information, the interpretation of the information is totally different. This is where you have to wear the hat of the psychotherapist. You can never assume that the information is heard or felt the same way from one person to the next. That is another way that I think the technicians blow it because they think, "The information is the information! Just the facts."

But it is the process of uncovering deeper meanings and emotions that have developed from profound hurts and unmet needs of the past that helps the social worker understand that being given news about your child's IQ can drive you to the brink of suicide. One father could want to get his gun and shoot himself because he learns that his son has a learning disability and an IQ of 85. Another family in that situation may say, "Oh, I'm so glad that he's not mentally retarded and we can do a lot with this." But you have to know that the first father had dyslexia in school and was in special education and was made to feel worthless by his family. Now, he feels that he has produced a similarly "defective" son, someone who is a reflection of his own unworthiness, and it is entirely his fault. I have a deep awareness that the information is being received by a unique individual who has a personality and a temperament, a lifetime history with a family, a culture, and adult life experiences that have played into it. In any given situation involving people, there are many interpretations and adaptations from being told the exact same information. But it is the social worker wearing the psychotherapist hat that knows this.

The third hat is that of an advocate. That is where the political process comes in because the emotional world of the family is not limited to a 50-minute hour. Even if you work on the information and the emotional psychotherapy part, clients have to live in a system of services. Unfortunately, the developmental disability system is a network of confusion and complexity. These families often have to deal with 10 different providers and systems, and they have to put it all together. They have to evaluate those services, get them paid for, and coordinate them. It can be a nightmare. A social worker knows how to help the family make decisions, get the professionals to work together, and then advocate for systems change.

Having a child is not like producing a factory product. From the time they learn of the pregnancy, parents fantasize about the child they will have. Proactive parents believe they will produce an offspring who is going to be beautiful and smart and not just as good as them but better. They think their child will be someone who will achieve things in this world—you know, "grow up to be president of the U.S." sort of thinking that a lot of people have as a fantasy. How well that child does in the world and how smart and productive he is will be a reflection back on the parents. They will give him their genes, raise him right, and shape and mold him. They will give him first-class education and all the benefits they can afford.

This is every parent's fantasy, but in the real world, I was working with families whose children were not attractive, were not achieving much, and who would never grow up to be president. Their parents knew all of this, and they loved them anyway. That was a profound lesson for me, that even disabled children are precious gifts who come into our lives, and our job is to love them and to help them reach their potential. These parents have taught me that helping a child who has an IQ of 50 learn independence skills is absolutely meaningful, good work, and it is worthy of our energy and attention. It is just as worthy as helping a gifted child learn a second language or play the violin.

I really believe in my heart that this is the true meaning of being a parent. Here is where my social work role comes in: When a family first has the diagnosis and realizes that the child is not going to be on this path of perfection and become a reflection of all their competence and their achievements in life, they really grieve. I accept the parents' grief because I know that they are losing their fantasy child, but I also have learned that there is life in the real world. Yes, there will be struggle and frustration, but there will also be love, and my joy is helping them understand this.

❖ **SUE BRANDT**

I became a social worker out of arrogance. I spent 12 years working with the profoundly handicapped. There was a kid in my classroom who I felt was being abused, and CPS (child protective services) was not doing what they should. Well, I can do better than them. I went down and applied. Lo and behold, I was hired, and here I am. I've been a supervisor for 8 years and before that was a worker for 7 years. I like the energy and excitement. I'm probably an adrenaline junkie.

The part of the job I like the best is the initial investigation—when you are dealing with new families and making the decision of whether the kids need to be removed from the home. Most of these clients don't have a lot of room for optimism once the children have been removed. When we take custody of the children and file a petition with the court, two-thirds of those children never go home again. Their parents never rebuild.

But when you work in investigation, you feel you have a certain level of success. If it's a bad situation and you have to remove the children, you've created, at least temporarily, a better situation for them. There is an immediateness: You're in, you're evaluating, and you're done. In investigation, we come across many families that never enter the system beyond us knocking on their door and talking with them and helping them get what they need. In these cases, we help keep the children in the home, and that is gratifying. It's not what the public hears about, but that is the bulk of the work we do, helping parents get what they need to take care of their kids.

Sometimes, it's very hard. I remember a kid named Christopher, a little 4-year-old, about 10 years ago. His mother's boyfriend almost burned and broiled the boy to death in hot water. He was in the hospital over a year. His genitals, his penis, were literally burned from his body. His body was fried. This guy tortured the kid for 2 weeks. This little boy was afraid of sirens, so he locked him in the closet and played a tape of sirens. He burned him at about 9 o'clock in the morning over 90% of his body. The only thing that wasn't burned was his head. He waited until about 8 at night to get help. It was one of the ugliest things I've ever experienced in my life . . . inconceivable. It was what made me believe in an automatic death penalty. That was ugly.

But sometimes, you have a more encouraging case, and you know why you stay. There was a young woman—17 and pregnant—who lived with her 28-year-old boyfriend. When her newborn was 17 days old, she stood there and watched her boyfriend beat him to death. The baby was shaken, he was bruised and battered, and he was laid down to die. When they finally took him to the hospital, he was DOA. They had no other children, but while they were pending trial, she got pregnant again. I removed that baby from the newborn nursery and placed him for adoption very quickly. Ultimately, she was convicted of lower-level felony child abuse, and he, of course, was convicted of murder. She went to prison for a short period of time, and she was on intensive probation. She struggled through. It was not an easy case at all. The sad part was she had come from a rough life herself.

Probably 3 years after I removed the second child, she came in and sat down next to me, stared at the wall, and said, "I'm pregnant, and I know you are going to take my baby." My immediate reaction was, "You bet I am." But she had made great strides. She had a tremendous probation officer, a person who really invested himself in her success. He was an older man, and he and his wife essentially adopted her and reparented her in a lot of ways. The baby's father was a very nice young man who was in the military. I didn't take the baby. I filed a petition for legal custody and provided legal supervision for that family for 5 years. She is now the mother of three little girls that are beautiful, bright, capable kids. She comes in probably three or four times a year and brings the kids by to see me. I would have never thought on my most optimistic day that she would have been able to do what she's done. She's really tremendous. I look at her kids, and if I leave this job never having done anything else, I know that she is raising those three girls with her husband. She is happily married, she's a great mom, and it's a tremendous feat.

It was not a popular decision. I certainly wasn't notorious as a person who gave a lot of chances. I've always been fairly hard-minded. We are not going to put kids at risk, we have to be sure. I'm not going to go home at night and let a kid be hurt because I underreacted. At the same time, I did it with a lot of supervision and support, and it fortunately turned out to be the right decision. I feel like that was a gift to me. I'm able to stand back and watch and say, "I had a part of that." But when you're doing this work, a case like this is a once-in-a-lifetime achievement. Small gifts like this you'd better hold on to.

You have to maintain a balance in your life if you're going to work for CPS. You have to remind yourself that not everybody is a child molester. Not everybody hits their kids. You have to kind of surround yourself with regular families and regular people so you remember regular people still exist.

From my own kids' perspective, they probably felt like there has always been too much work to do and too little time. It's not like I'm working on the assembly line at IBM and if I make a mistake, somebody's computer doesn't work. If I make a mistake here or I cut a corner there and I don't get something done, a child can die, a child can be maimed. This is a level of responsibility that I think made my kids sometimes resent me. When they were small children and I was an investigator, they got real tired of their grandmother coming to pick them up from day care or after school because I had to work late. But if it is 5:00 p.m. and a child discloses that their father is having sex with them, you don't say, "Gee, I have to get my kids out of day care, so I'll come back tomorrow." For a case like this, I may have to work until 1:00 a.m.

There are certainly more pleasant, cleaner, less smelly kinds of social work. I think, unfortunately, a lot of workers want to come in and fix these families. That is not our job. Our job is to provide parents with the tools and the opportunities they need. But ultimately, our job is to go home every night and know that everything we put our hands on for today is OK.

We have a tendency to lose sight of why we get that first phone call: The first phone call is because a child is at risk. Imagine that you get a call from a child's school and go to the kid's school and you call him into the office. You establish rapport, and you delve into the ugliest aspects of his life. Within 45 minutes, you have to make a decision. You have to be tremendously respectful of that brief opportunity. You can say, "Well, I've had a bad day. I've fought with my husband. I've fought with my wife. I've fought with my kids." Yeah, you did, but you better find a way to do your job because if you blow your one shot, it's not like somebody's getting a bad computer. If this is the work that you chose to do, you have to recognize that when a child talks to you, that is a gift, and you better make full use of the gift. Don't just leave it unopened because you are tired or having a bad day.

I continuously remind myself not to become objective, not to become remote, not to lose my humanity. If it ever gets to the point that what I do doesn't bother me anymore, then I'll know it's time to leave. If what I see doesn't make me sad, I don't belong here because, no matter what, it is always sad to take a child away from his parents. You can't lose sight of the fact that no matter how bad the parents seem to you, these children love their parents. I've never been with a kid yet who said, "Take me away." What they say is, "Get my parent to stop doing … (fill in the blank) … and then we can go back home." You have to always remember, children want to be home. And sometimes, they just don't get to go back home, and that is so sad. I hope I always think this way.

This work has made me cynical about different systems, cynical about society's capacity to do what is right for people. But at the same time, you know it depends on the day, it depends on the hour. I don't know anyone who works in CPS who is honest who hasn't felt that they can't see one more case. If you work for more than a year, you go through an annual cycle of "This was a huge mistake and why am I here?" You kind of struggle your way through it, and you come back around. If you want to survive and you want to continue to do good work, you have to bring a balance back around. I see it in the workers about once a year, at different times of the year for each one of them: "I hate this job. Why do I work here?" But I suspect that is true no matter what type of job you have. I think that everyone finds their niche in life to some degree, and it doesn't matter where you work, you go through periods of, "This was a bad choice."

I still like coming to work everyday. I have an opportunity to do what I think is very important. These are tiny people who don't have a lot going for them and don't have a lot of people watching out for them. But some of them have me.

❖ ANDREA KUSHNER

Growing up in my family, I always felt that I had to talk quickly in order to get information out because people's attention span when they were listening to me was short. People weren't emotionally or psychologically invested in what was going on with me. I felt that people had a right to be heard and a right to be listened to. I wanted to provide people with the opportunity to speak and express their emotions and their feelings in a place where they were going to be heard. That's what got me into social work. I wanted to help people who aren't heard in their lives and who come from circumstances in which they haven't even been seen. Incarcerated people are an unheard, unseen population. They don't have a lot of privileges, and they don't have a lot of rights, for a variety of reasons. I felt the need to get out there and give people half a chance, especially juveniles. Maybe I felt like they still had a chance if they got help.

These kids have taught me a lot. Each of them in their own individual way has impacted me. I've had a hard time separating myself from the ones who allow themselves to feel pain the most and who had emotional breakdowns in my office. They have been in a tremendous amount of pain. I just want to take these kids and shelter and protect them from any more harm. You just want to take them home sometimes and set up a new life for them, but you can't. You can't come in and save the day. You can't come in and say, "I'm going to erase the last 14, 15, 16, 17 years of your life and make it all better for you." Those are the kids that you struggle with because you know that their journey is going to be long, and they've got a lot of healing ahead of them. But they are fighters and survivors. These kids are still going, they're still alive, and they are still taking care of themselves. They are still, in a lot of ways, treating themselves with respect, treating others with respect, and treating their relationships with respect. It's been horrible, but my God, they are still standing and still fighting this battle, and you've got to have a ton of respect for them.

Social work is not necessarily therapy. You're in the environment helping people. You're not just sitting behind a desk talking to people. You are consistently, proactively, going out to meet people's needs. That is what your job is. It's to meet people's needs as best you can and help them internalize so they can eventually carry on without you.

That is the goal of treatment, to eventually wean people off of it so they can get on with their own lives and have a strong enough sense of self. For that, you need to utilize resources. You need to utilize yourself, you need to utilize other people, and you need to utilize the environment. You can't do it with one of those lacking.

The treatment relationship isn't about you, it's about them. You become part of their world, and you work on their stuff in your relationship with them. It's never about you, and it's never about burdening your client with any of your stuff. You have to be real careful and always walk a real fine boundary line to make sure that you empathically can get into their world, but you also can remove yourself from their world at any time to offer objectivity and to offer a sense of distance. If you offer too much distance, it becomes a problem, and if you get too involved it becomes a problem, which is why you always have to be finding that fine line. You need to somehow engage yourself in their world and think about, "What is it like to be this person?" Not, "What is it like for me to observe this person?" In order to do that, sometimes you have to get into their world, but if you become part of their helplessness and hopelessness, you become stuck with them. If you're stuck with them, you are no good to yourself or to them. You need to have one foot in and one foot out at all times. Without that foot, you have nothing to stand on.

There should be no personal agenda for the therapist. The agenda for the therapist is to sit and do the best they can in trying to understand that other person, whether they are moving in centimeters, inches, feet, or yards. You need to be there, wherever they are. That is a huge thing that I've learned, because everybody is in a different place, and people suffering from different symptoms move more gradually or have more or less insight or can step away from a problem better than others. Some people don't have that capacity, and that is something that you have to go back and work on.

You have to make sure that you are going into a treatment setting in a relatively clear frame of mind. That means every day making sure that you're OK and that you're not going to be taking out your own stuff into the relationship because you can't do that. That calls for you to work on yourself, but also know every day that you are not perfect. You're not a saint, and you are going to run into troubles and obstacles and barriers in your life just like everybody else. You are going to need to somehow separate your personal stuff from the relationship, always and every day, because it's not fair to bring it in. It's not fair to the client. It's not fair to the relationship. I have to understand that I'm not going to have a great day every day. I'm not going to feel that I'm ready to go in there every day and solve all these problems, but I'm going to be able to do the best that I can. Doing the best that you can every moment is hard sometimes, especially when you are going through whatever is coming up in your own life. You can learn to separate it.

It can be frustrating. Social workers have to work within the social system. You don't always find that the people who work in that system are doing the best job they can to help your client. It's not so much that I get frustrated with the kids as I get frustrated with services that they should be getting, and they are not. When somebody is put into the hands of a person who is not doing their job, that is the most frustrating. These kids put their confidence into people who are supposed to be taking care of them, and they fail them.

I try to trust the process. You have to. You have to trust the process and to some extent the system. If you start losing faith in that, then the whole thing collapses. There are people who it hasn't been fair to, but there are a lot of people where the system has worked for them, and they have moved on with their lives and gotten out. They have gotten what they need in some way, shape, or form that was good enough to allow them to become psychologically stable people. You have to trust that. You have to trust the good people out there who do take this to heart and are ethical and do their job. If you stay focused on the people and entities in the systems that don't, you are going to run yourself into the ground. You have to have faith in your supervisors and faith in the system and how it works. You have to know the flaws and the problems, but overall, in general, we have to maintain some sort of positive respect for what is going on.

You aren't going to see immediate results. It's not, "What you put into it is what you get out of it." You usually aren't going to be able to go home at the end of the day and say, "OK, that's over now, and I'm going to move to the next thing tomorrow." It's a constant learning process, and you are never fully done with it—ever. From the first day you begin as a social worker until the day before you retire, it's never a finished process; it's always a continuous flow of helping people. There is not a lot of the closure that some people need. Some people who aren't in social work need to see a project finished. They need to see the finished product, and they need to say, "Here you go. This is the fruit of your labor." That is not something that you can get. I think social workers need to understand that.

I think, for people that aren't social workers, it's hard to understand the treatment relationship. A professor of mine said to me in a Psychotherapy of Adults class, "You know, friends and family—and you can't be disappointed by this—will never truly understand what you do. They'll never truly understand it, and you can't expect them to." People are not stagnant. They don't present themselves in the same way week after week with the same sorts of problems. I think that is something somebody from the outside would have difficulty tolerating, that consistent changing and consistent moving. The social worker has to adjust to circumstances: lack of resources, lack of money, lack of appreciation.

You have to make sure that you are in social work for the right reasons and not to work on yourself in any way. It's a big commitment, and you need to know the reality of being a social worker. You need to understand yourself and get your issues sorted out. That is something that you need to be committed to, first and foremost. If you are not committed to that, then I don't think you should be in the field. You should be committed to the idea of helping people, period. Social workers don't have a magic wand that they can wave and everything is going to be better. Most of the work is going to have to be done by other people. The object is to give them the tools to do that: to allow them to do it for themselves so they feel valued, worthwhile, and have enough self-esteem to build themselves up into the kind of person who is able to take care of themselves psychologically so they are not in so much pain. You can't do the work for them. You can be with them in the process, and you can help guide them, but the work is on the person. That is the bottom line. Self-empowerment is one of the principles of social work practice, making people feel like they can and do have the strength to do what they need to do to take care of themselves. I think that is a process that they learn. It comes with patience and having a sense of worth.

2

A Meaningful Path

❖ **MELINDA OLIVER**

Yesterday, I went to the funeral of an elderly woman who I'd been involved with for about 8 years. It was a small crowd, mostly people who had cared for her. Even her housekeeper was there. This woman had outlived all of her peers. Everyone had died and she had nobody left, yet at the viewing yesterday, it was kind of a happy time. We had some laughs about what an irascible old woman she was and how she lived life by her own standards. In her declining years, she had fought every step of the way and managed to preserve her dignity. I knew that we had helped her to achieve her goal. She had lived life on her own terms, and we had enabled her to have her dignity. I see that as my role, to help people live a good life until it's time to die. Yesterday, it struck home in my heart—this is the purpose of what I'm doing. It is to give people a good life. To help them in whatever way that I can when they are not physically able to do it for themselves. To help them as they grow older and more frail.

In my work, I act as a family member for people who have no family. I work through the court systems with guardianships and conservatorships. It really is life involvement. It's the progression until death. When we started with this woman, she was living in her own home, and we helped her through an appropriate placement, and we managed to keep her life good up until she died. She had one niece who truly cared about her, and this niece came and sprinkled her aunt's ashes off of Mt. Lemmon to the tones of Beethoven, the music booming and the ashes flying. She came back and brought me a single flower and gave me a big hug and said, "Thank you for making her life so good when I couldn't be here." It was touching because this woman almost outlived her money. She was 97 when she died. She was down to a pitiful amount of money and could not afford the nursing home much longer but still had a good life up until the day she died. I felt successful in that case because when you are 97 and you've had a good life and your money is ready to go and your life is ready to change radically, it's OK to die.

Some of my elderly clients are so trusting, so trusting it's scary. A lot of the times, Adult Protective Services calls us in because they realize there is an exploitation problem. I've walked in, and they've given me their bank statements, their bank books, their bills ... everything that is important to them. I mean, they just hand me the checkbook and say, "Here, look at this. I'm having trouble with it." They don't know who I am. I could be anybody. That happens over and over and over again. They'll hand me a stack of papers, and that is part of my job, to go in and gather them up. We have legal authority to do it, to go in and gather up bills and important papers, documents, so they can be protected. The bills can be paid so the utilities are not turned off. But to have that woman, that person, not know who I am and to turn all that stuff over to me ... I'm just glad that I'm the person.

It's common for people to take advantage of the elderly. We've had people try to change elderly people's wills. Take them to attorneys when they are obviously incompetent, to try to get themselves on the will. Or there'll be a conflict of interest where someone is appointed guardian of an individual who is a recipient in the will, and they try to preserve the estate and do the least amount possible for that individual so that they will make more money when the person dies. That happens in a lot of our cases. We see so many of the elderly who are being taken advantage of. I've seen people jump for joy when an elderly relative dies, thinking they are going to be covered in the will. I'm kind of glad when they are not.

Sometimes, we get the people that nobody else wants because they are so difficult that others wash their hands of them. Nobody cares about them anymore because they are mean or nasty, but they still need protection. We are the office of last resort where people just dump older people who they can't deal with. I had one client in particular who had me in tears many, many times because she was so mean to me. She threw rocks at me. She threw water on me. She locked me in the house and pushed me down. She was in her 80s, and she was strong. She wouldn't let me leave her house, and I told her, "If you don't let me leave your house, I'm going to call 911." She'd call me up and cuss at me with nasty profanity on the phone. I'd either hang up on her, or she would get disgusted and hang up on me. She was fighting getting old and losing her sense of power. All her power was being taken away from her, and I was one of the people taking it. I was representing a lot more than just myself. I was the focus of all this nastiness because she was losing her ability to live alone and hated it. Oh, she made life miserable for me. I dreaded coming to work in that time because she would torment me.

But I had a responsibility to keep her safe. I would get in her house and then she'd get angry. I would talk my way into her house because I needed to see what she had in her refrigerator. I wanted to see if she was safe, if she was forgetting to turn off the burners on the stove. She had put a bottle of bleach in her refrigerator because it was in the same shape of a carton of milk. I needed to see those kinds of things in order to keep her safe, to not drink the bleach. That bleach actually was the turning point when she needed to be removed from her home. She knew she was borderline but couldn't admit it. She knew that she was no longer safe, but she was fighting it every step of the way. But that is not an unusual situation in our line of work, to have people who are so angry at their loss of so many things in life, and they need a scapegoat, and we're the scapegoat.

She's not angry with me. She's angry at the loss of ability. It does get to me sometimes. It's hard not to take it personally when it's a constant barrage of cut downs. We have a supportive office here, and we get together every week and discuss all the cases. We look at it as a group and discuss how we could have changed things and what were our successes and what were our failures. We talk about how we can improve the way that we deal with the next person based on what we did with the last. This is a cohesive group of people who get along well and support each other, and that makes all the difference in the world.

The hardest case for me was the death of a child. He was 3 years old. This was a major life event for me. It made me take a deep breath and think about how I approach things. I didn't think this child was going to die. I encouraged the mother in what I thought at the time was a positive way. I didn't think this child would die. I was flabbergasted that he died. His mother knew he was going to die, but I felt he had a chance at a good life. I probably said all the wrong things to her. I thought at the time that I was encouraging her but in retrospect, maybe what I was doing was giving her false hope, giving myself false hope. His mother knew he was dying, but I couldn't face that fact. At the viewing, she couldn't keep her hands off the child. She was rubbing him, patting him, and rearranging his hair and kissing him and holding him. He was in the casket, but she just couldn't let go of this child. It was distressing to me because I felt like instead of listening to her talk about her dying child, I had kind of poo-pooed her and gave her my own opinions so I didn't have to face his death. My opinions weren't appropriate. This experience changed my listening skills. I don't offer opinions anymore, and I tend to really listen now. That is part of growing as a social worker.

❖ **LINDA BOLES**

I'm an advocate for social change. I want to change the world and make it a safer place. I work as the advocate in a small, rural community. That means that I provide support groups, domestic violence counseling, transfer to shelters, transport to courts, legal advocacy, social services, referrals for all of the county. I drive around in the car a lot. My day gets split up between doing a lot of education with cops, fire departments, EMTs (emergency medical teams), animal control, so that everybody is on the same page. We are trying to get more shelter services. We are trying to get more money for transitional housing programs and trying to see what the rural communities need. I've always been a feminist and worked at battered women's shelters. In this job, I feel like, "I'm home. I've found the right niche."

I think that doing social work is a challenge. In the nonprofit world, there is this kind of myth of, "Here is your job description." Then you get hired and it's, "Oh, by the way, we are going to tack on A, B, and C."

Then, there is this expectation that you're going to do it since we are all part of the Cause. I don't think a lot of the nonprofit sector is conducive to maintaining good health. The salaries are low. The caseloads are high. Some days, I think, "Oh, cosmetics at Dillard's—I'll go sell cosmetics at Dillard's." I joke about it on a daily basis because it is really crazy. I do believe in the Cause. Coming from a background of domestic violence in my own life probably motivates me.

I work for the victims. But say for example that dad is the abuser, I'll work with mom and the kids; but if dad isn't plugged into the system, I'll work with him for a few sessions to at least get him plugged in. You have to treat all the family members with compassion and kindness, even the perpetrators. I'm not saying that I'm supporting men who are violent or women who are violent, but they're human beings and they have emotions and feelings, and I think what they do is nuts and it's illegal and they're going to get locked away, but you're still a person and you need treatment. If I don't deal with dad, he might dump this wife and get remarried and start doing it again.

I also work with kids who have to be removed from the home because of child protective services. They are sitting in my car crying because they have to leave for the seventh time in 6 months. I'm like, "This has got to stop." It's not going to happen in my lifetime or several lifetimes from now, but you know this is not OK. A lot of people don't know it's not legal for me to put my hands on you without your permission. Well, why? They say, "When I was a kid, my father slapped me around, and I turned out OK." A lot of my work is changing people's minds: "Well, Mr. Smith, perhaps there might be a more effective way to do that and get the same results without the bruises."

Sometimes, I think I'm not going back, but then I have a special case, and I realize how important this work is. I recently talked to a woman on the phone, and she seemed to be in crisis. I do the lethality assessment. There are no drugs. There are no weapons in the house. There is no alcohol. One thing I didn't ask was how jealous he is. I blew it. I made a mistake. I didn't assess how obsessive he was. I could hear him in the background. "Tell her about the cop you slept with. Tell her about the cop you slept with." I just had a funny feeling, and I hung up the phone and I called the Sheriff's department, and I said, "Look. I don't know. I've got a funny feeling, so just go out and check for me." The woman drives off. The man disappears and comes back with a gun. He gets in his car and is driving down the road to kill this lady. He has a firearm at this point and tries to shoot her in the head. She manages to swerve and gets on the cell phone and calls 911. There were 80 hairs from her head attached to that bullet. According to everything the docs said, she should have been dead. Had I not called the police … I could have lost her. One of these days, I will lose a client, and I don't want to screw up.

It's very hard to maintain the balance. In the domestic violence arena when you are dealing with suicides and homicides and all kinds of stuff, it's not like, "Oh, I'm having trouble at school and my eyes are red from studying all night." It's more like, "Oh, he put his hand around my neck and choked me so hard, and now my eyes are all red because they are full of blood."

You have to have a really good sense of humor. I do things to take care of myself: no dark movies; happy, funny, sitcoms; limit the newspapers. You have to laugh every single day. That is my goal. Tell me a funny joke. Call my answering machine, it says, "Hi. We're not in; please leave a joke," because you have to laugh. Otherwise, I think I would give up my faith in humanity.

Off and on, I've been doing this for 10 years, and about every 3 years, I take a break. One summer, I folded shirts at a golf shop. That was very good, rewarding. Another summer, I went back to Indonesia and taught middle-level managers to speak English. Anybody who has been in social work for any extended period of time who doesn't take a break, I think they are really nuts. There are some people in this field, particularly in the domestic violence arena, who say, "I've been doing this for 20 years." I'm like, "Yeah, and how are you doing?"

I've seen an increase in social work. We are returning to embracing the spirit. There's that whole sense of what is going on in our society and people are trying to figure it out and solve it. We couldn't talk about domestic violence in the '60s. It was very underground. If you talked about it before then, it was very hush hush. We have made progress. I'd love to see what it's going to look like in another 20 to 25 years. I think more people are interested in trying to get to the root of the problem. That's about it. Got any good jokes?

❖ JOYCE MORGAN

I was 12 when I left home and ended up in a runaway shelter. And then I ended up in another shelter, and then an orphanage. Then I was a foster child and realized everything before had been really, really bad. It was the reverse of what most children in foster care experience. They say they get in the system and it ruins their life. I never looked at it that way. I looked at the system and the people involved in the system as giving me life.

One lady I knew in particular was what you'd call the ideal, unbelievable, perfect social worker. She could talk to you, and there could be 40 people trying to get her attention, but you were the center of her world. I remember her today. God gave her a gift, and through that gift, I decided what to be. I'll never be her because I didn't get that gift that she has. She was awesome. She is still awesome. That is how I became a social worker. I was never unhappy with my choice. I always just thought, this is where I belong.

As of tomorrow, I am the family services coordinator supervisor for the Department of Juvenile Corrections. Which means I supervise five social workers in five different parole offices across two counties. I've been doing this work for about 10 years. I've always worked with kids. That's not a true statement—I've always worked with kids and families. You can't work with the kid without the family.

Before you get to know the kids we work with, you see them like everyone else does. You know—"How awful, how tragic, why would they do that?" And then you meet them. I remember a 13-year-old who shot and killed his best friend. You hear the story, and you think, "Oh how awful and how horrible." Then, you meet the kid, and you think, "What a little boy." And you try to put the two together. What happened is never exactly what the plan was. Something got out of control. Something went off. He did something that not only destroyed his best friend but destroyed him. Whoever he was supposed to be, he can't be that anymore. You have two tragedies. Occasionally, I hear that you will meet someone who kills and just doesn't care. I guess those kids are out there; I have never met one. Usually, when you get behind why they killed somebody, you find out that they're kids, and they're lost. And they're more lost than we are. I won't tell you that they won't kill again, I can't even guarantee that they'll ever change, but right now, they are kids and we created them and they are our kids.

We allow our children to be raised in unholy, horrible, negative, disastrous environments, and we don't protect them. We remove children from horrible, disastrous families, and we place them in an equally horrible system. Group homes are the most frustrating. You have children; you take them from their homes and then you make them live by rules that would make us, as adults, scream and pull out our hair. You put them in a group home and say, "Be children here. But be out of bed by this time. Make your bed by this time. If you don't, you lose points." You have just put them in a little group home jail. And you've said, "Now, be happier here because no one is beating you." Well, maybe they're not beating him, but now he lives in a prison that we call a group home. And he's still being punished over and over.

When I was in an orphanage, they had rules, but we really just grew up. I mean, they had structure, but it wasn't like today. You know, today we criminalize kids in the foster care system. You call the cops because they're a half-hour late for curfew. I don't know a kid in America that hasn't ever gotten home late from school.

We take damaged children, put them in an oppressive environment, continue to make them feel bad about who they are, and then we ask them why they go to prison. It's because we victimize them. There are a few special foster homes out there, and the kids in those homes are blessed. But that's not our system. Every once in a while, you run into those homes, and you think, "Thank you, God." But most of the time, I walk into these homes and think, "Came from hell and now he lives in a new hell." Before long, he runs from there, and he goes right into the cycle of violence and crime and gangs. That's where he comes from. That's where he's safe.

But if you're positive and you respect who they are—even if you don't agree with who they are—it may be 3 years, it might be 5 years, you might never know, but you can touch them. If you take a physically abused kid and you discipline them by yelling, screaming, being the hardcore "gonna make you do what I tell you" then you just abuse him some more. But if you're gentle and you just treat him like a person—someday he is going to remember that you treated him OK. It may not be measurable or definable, but you can touch kids. All you've got to do is treat them like humans and not continue to do what was done to them. I don't know that you fix or change kids, but if you don't hurt them, then when they get older, they can look back and feel good about you. So do no harm. Don't be abusive. Don't be mean. Listen to them.

I'm a realist, and I don't have a candy attitude about anything. I don't believe that I control the destiny of any kid or situation. I can't control their lives. I can't control their outcomes. I can't control their destinies or their fate. And I really believe in luck. 'Cause there but for the grace of God go me. Why me and why not you? Whatever his cards were dealt, they were his cards. You know that old philosophy question, "Do you control your destiny or does your destiny control you?" I believe destiny controls you to some extent. One day, you're healthy, the next you're sicker than a dog. Why you? One day, your life's perfect, and the next day, you wreck your car. Why you? Some people believe you control your own destiny. I don't. Why me, why do I get to have a nice life? I don't mean that I'm always happy and think it's wonderful, but most of the time I'm content. But why did I get that? I have a brother who was raised with me who lives a life of hell. Why? I didn't do anything special to get to be where I was. I look at kids the same way. Here's one kid who has horrible circumstances, horrible parents, the worst things you can imagine, and he graduates from high school and goes on. This kid right next to him—same circumstances, same life—he spends his life in prison. Did he choose that, as a choice?

I help them the best I can. But I think what I struggle with most is the process. I struggle every day because from where I sit, it's so easy for me to see the direction. The hardest thing that I do is to get kids to go there. I can know where they need to go, but to find the path for them to get there is the hard part. God gave me insight and incredible clinical skills. I can diagnose anybody. I can see the problem clearly. Sometimes, I can get them to get where they need to be, but just as often, I struggle with why they can't get there. I'm completely comfortable with whatever my population is. Connecting with them takes 4 seconds. Empathy and all that kind of stuff I don't have a problem with. But I don't always know how to get someone to go through a process and to see an outcome and to be successful. I want it as badly as you could want anything on the planet. I want it like you want a Christmas present that's the biggest box under the tree. I want to open it up and get the process so that any child I touch, I could lead them and they would go. I talked before about my friend. She had that gift. She'd lead a kid anywhere. I want that gift.

This work has very much changed my perception of the world. I see more violence in a day than most people see in a lifetime. I see more hatred in a day than most people see in forever. I ride down the streets, the person next to me sees people shopping and milling around. I see gang bangers, drug dealers, car thieves, prostitutes. I'm driving, and I don't see the nice little old man helping the lady. I see the guy over there stealing the woman's car.

Yet I like the people I work with. I meet some amazing moms who are just incredible, wonderful people who awe me—they have such grace and spirit. I respect them, and I'm in awe of them, but I don't need to go home with them and have dinner with them. I have no problem with boundaries. I have clients who call me years after I've done therapy with them or worked with their kids. I have some who want to be my friend, and I have to give this little speech: "I was your therapist. That puts us on an unequal footing. I can't become your friend."

I think that every day you make choices about what kind of person you are going to be. I know social work gave me that choice because my upbringing taught me all about the other side. I know all those people on the other side. I know how they live. I know about violence. I know about everything out on the street. And I got to make a choice because I knew about social work. And many, many, many people don't get to make that choice. It was a gift to become a social worker. It still is my gift.

❖ MICHAEL PESCE

When I think about how I got into social work and particularly into child welfare, I think a lot about how my mother grew up. She spent a good deal of her childhood in an orphanage. Her father died when she was 3 years old and left her mother with a bunch of kids. In order to survive, she kept some of them and sent some of them away, and my mother was one of the ones sent away. Throughout my childhood, I heard about the impact of not having a consistent home. Not having unconditional presence. Not having someone to count on. I think that impacted me unconsciously for a long time.

I wanted to change the world. I would have gone into politics if I thought you could legislate love. Oh God, now it sounds corny, but if you could legislate good things, maybe people would be good. My interest in government stemmed from service to people. While I was still in college, I started doing some work and independent study in child welfare issues and juvenile justice. I liked that. At the time, I didn't know any social workers. I took a class in social welfare, and I remember a professor saying, "Oh, people do social work just for a little while and then they go and sell real estate."

In spite of this encouraging information, I went to graduate school and had a field placement where I worked with the State Department of Social Services in the area of foster care. I've been in foster care and adoption ever since; it fits perfectly with the issues from my childhood. I've done administrative work, worked with the juvenile court systems. I did direct service for 4 years doing casework and then 4 years recruiting families for the foster care system. Then after that, I worked with some private agencies doing foster care work in more of a supervisory or program development position. I was a social work supervisor, and now I've become the director. That's over 20 years of doing social work. I love it. It feeds me. It satisfies me.

I still go back to the core thing. I need to do something that matters—that matters to somebody else and that matters to me, something that has value. That is a demonstration of caring. That comes in many ways. It could be a one-to-one thing with a kid or a family. It could be advocating. In my current position, I'm doing even more community work, more advocacy. When I think back, that is originally why I went into social work.

It all wasn't roses. I remember once looking at a case and thinking, "Oh God. I'd hate to get this case." Later that afternoon, I came back and it's sitting on my desk. An African American woman who was mentally ill had killed one of her twin children, and the body was so badly decomposed, they couldn't determine the cause of death. They never prosecuted her, though. She hated men and she hated white people. So, voila! Me, this white guy, ends up with this case.

She was horrible. I would supervise visits with her kids. She would arrange the chairs so that the kids couldn't have eye contact with me. She never referred to me by name. She would always refer to me by my position number. She hated me. There was no way to work with her. She consistently referred to me as a liar, and I had to go to court every time there was any little thing going on. It was just harassment; it was a nightmare. She would talk to her kids and tell them how white men would force black women to get pregnant and then force them to have abortions by jumping on their stomachs—horrible things, just absolutely horrible things. I went to work and I said, "I can't do this anymore. This is not me. This is way past what I can handle. I need to get out of this."

This case made me think about leaving the field, and it wasn't the last time I thought this. Even now sometimes, I think, "Am I getting out of this what I want to?" The answer is yes. The answer has always been yes. Even during this awful case, it was yes.

There are millions of other stories that have great meaning to me. Like when kids look at you and they know that you care about them. They hear that you are on their side and that you understand them, that you care about them. I think back to that time when I went out and took these kids out of a foster home where there had been some abuse, and this little kid looked at me and said, "Thank you." And you go, "Wow! This is what this is about." That's not a big gigantic success story, but it was a moment that I have never forgotten.

We talk so much about outcomes. Outcomes are important, but relationships are important, too. And processes are really important, sometimes more important, because the reality is that we have limited influence over outcomes, but we have a lot of input into how we make relationships and how we set up processes. I've been critical about what is a success. It's not what I think, it's what somebody else thinks will be valuable to them in their eyes, like raising kids to be healthy, responsible, confident young adults. Well, what does that mean to them? To me, success doesn't just mean that you graduate high school and go to college and get a real high-paying job. Some people call that success. Maybe success is that I work at Wal-Mart, but I'm not an alcoholic like my father. Or I didn't pick a partner who abuses me. Or when I have a kid, I'll be able to make a better decision about how to take care of him. I think that's great success.

This may sound kind of rosy, but I still think there is good inside of everybody. I sound like somebody who is 21 years old. But you know what? People have to be who they are going to be, and you do the best that you can. If you can find a way to bring that goodness out, even if for a little tiny bit of time ... I work in an area where a lot of times, people think birth parents are terrible people. Yeah, there are drugs and there are other things, other pressures and all the other stuff that create people. People don't really choose to be crazy. People don't choose to be drug addicts and go, "Oh, I think I'd like to be a drug addict when I grow up." It happens. It happens for any number of reasons. It could happen to any one of us.

Sometimes, when we do the "them" and the "us" bit, we build this great abyss between us. We are not so different. Who is to say that things couldn't happen and I couldn't be homeless or I couldn't go through a severe depression. I could have a psychotic episode. It could happen to any of us. That's an important thing to remember. We are just people. Remember the people stuff. I try to do that. That doesn't mean that I don't have my human times when I get pissed off at people, and I think they are weirdos and wonder why are they coming here. But when I can be in sane times and when I can see clearly, I see the good.

For example, if a birth parent is not a good influence, is frequently drunk, or is in jail, or whatever, we think, "what good thing could they give their kid?" But maybe they write them a poem or maybe they buy them socks. Maybe if that's all they could ever do, then a kid grows up saying, "You know, my mom, she always bought me socks." Children can love parents even when they are a bad influence. Instead, we just cut between them and say this is good and this bad. That doesn't make any sense. There is nothing that simple: good parent, bad parent. I'm always amazed at how much we want to believe that it's that simple, maybe because it's easier to deal with it that way.

I had been told early on in my career that I was supposed to go and fix things. "Go fix this family. Go fix this kid. Go fix this problem." Well, that's not what we do. As social workers, we are not powerful people. We are not integral in changing people's lives. We are not the experts. We are none of those things. We are just the facilitators of the process so that people find their own way and do what they need to do. We may guide them. We may nudge them. We may coach them. We may be their cheerleader. We may walk with them. But it's all about what they want, not about what we want. When I got that, all of a sudden, I felt the weight lift right off of me. It was like, "Oh, who told me that I ever had to fix people?"

A director of an agency once told me, "I know a lawyer, a corporate lawyer, and he said, 'You guys in child welfare are never going to sit at the table of the power people.' I used to get angry and go, 'How come we are at the bottom of the pole? We work with poor, abused, mentally ill people, isn't that important?'" Our society doesn't value those people, so it doesn't value those who work with them. I used to get angry about it, and now it's part of what I embrace. Society wants us to keep them quiet, keep them out of the newspaper, keep them out of our homes. Then, everything will be fine. You just get to the point and go, "Well, that's the way it is." I know the limits of my advocacy. I'm not going to change the world so that all of a sudden kids and families become the number one priority in our country. Can I chip away at it? Sure. Can I make a difference in a small way? Sure.

One of the things that I said for a long time about this work is you have to learn to pat yourself on the back. I still have not shaken that. I still look at something that I do and go, "I did good." To be able to say, "Alright. I did a good piece of work," that is my bottom line. It goes back to the same thing, which is still the core of why I do this: I remember my mother wanting a consistent home. And then, I remember that it's important to make contributions. It's important to give. It's important to try to make things better for people.

3

Passion for Justice

❖ ANITA ROYAL

Being a child of the '60s, I was influenced by the antiwar demon-strations, the war on poverty, the Johnson Administration, and the Civil Rights Movement. I became interested in the plight of juveniles and the juvenile justice system. But my father believed that all his children should have accounting degrees, so he signed me up as a business major. I realized within a year that is not where my heart was. I changed to social work and have loved it ever since.

After doing social work for a while, I saw that social workers were not really respected and were not able to bring about institutional change. I needed a lot more power. I believed that if I became a lawyer, I could effect some real system change. I was still this naive product of the '60s thinking we could all change the world. A law degree became what was most important to me. Unfortunately, I learned that the law is set up to train people who are going into private practice. After law school, I ended up a public defender. But I see myself as a lawyer and a social worker. I use my social work skills as much as I use legal skills.

What is different between sociologists, psychiatrists, and social workers is that social workers are social engineers. We are the architects of society. We are the ones who can go out and do the programmatic changes and the policy changes. We are here to look at how society and the community fit together, to identify what barriers exist for people. How can we address those barriers and help people to be productive members of society?

We need to emphasize with future social workers the need for large-scale reform because without policy change, we will continue to languish as we are, with the haves and the have-nots and the functioning and the dysfunctioning segments of our society. Social workers need to know how to draft a bill, get it through a committee, and get it approved. How to get a referendum on the ballot so that we can make some changes. Get the news out to people. Get people in our communities organized. We are seeing in Washington and in our state capitals that we are balancing our budgets on the backs of poor people, and the middle class is paying for it. The rich are getting richer. The middle class is much more vulnerable. Even in two-parent homes, we are seeing more of an alienation of members of the family. We are seeing people break apart. There needs to be a renewed commitment to social advocacy, social justice, and policy change on a wide scale.

This is the reason why I love social work: to be able to say that we have made things better. We, social workers, are the leaders of this change of making things better. It is disturbing to me to see a lot of lawyers making decisions about people's welfare, especially since legal education does not focus on human beings. Law students don't take a class called Law and Human Behavior or Law and Social Change. Yet what is the law really dealing with? People's problems. Do you want people who don't have backgrounds in human behavior solving people's problems?

Being involved with children gives a lot of balance to my life. Working with Head Start lets me see the brightness and the hope in children of 3 and 4 years of age. There is potential in that population that no one really cares about. Who really cares about poor children? But you can see them develop and grow, and you see this whole system of teachers, health educators, and family educators that surrounds and embraces these families.

In terms of the plight of the elderly, I don't see any change coming anytime soon. The job I have now in the Public Fiduciary's office is the most challenging job I've ever had. I deal with the most vulnerable segment of our population every day, day in, day out—the elderly, a population that can't speak for itself. Right now for instance, we are simply inundated with financial exploitation of the elderly. The FBI is getting involved, and U.S. attorneys across the country are getting involved, but you do not see the national response that you do to child abuse. I believe that this is just the beginning, though, and it's coming as the baby boomers age.

Everyone is exploiting the elderly: family members, institutions, caretakers, real estate people, financial planners, the shopping channel. A family member or friend gets an elderly person to sign a power of attorney, and the next thing you know, there is $200,000 missing. Or a caretaker comes in and befriends the homebound person, and the next thing you know, the will has changed, leaving everything to the home health aide. Or the priest needs more money and $250,000 is suddenly missing, and the priest is the sole beneficiary of the will—or the minister, or the nurse. There are children who believe their parent's money is their money. At some point in time, they are going to inherit it anyway, so why not take some cash gifts now. I think part of this is the breakdown of the family where we don't have other members of our family around being watchdogs. I don't see families with a lot of support right now. What I see is a whole lot of older people isolated and alone.

I had a case where a woman died in her house. We found a bunch of empty wine bottles but no water in the house. She had a son who died in the house in the middle of the summer. We didn't find him for 2 or 3 weeks, so the body had liquefied. Where was the family? She must have been living like this for years. It didn't happen overnight. Where was that family?

What about the people who haven't talked to their children in 35 years? And then we call the children and say, "We have your mother and she has dementia" or "Your father has dementia," and we hear, "I'm sorry but I'm not going to be there." What is going on? Is life so difficult that we can't bring aid to our loved ones in their time of need? In this job, you begin to think about the important things in life. I always tell my friends and everyone I know that you never, never want to get that estranged from a family member. I don't care what has happened in the past. As you become adults, forgive your parents. You only get one set of parents; you didn't ask for them, you got them. You forgive them for who they were as parents as you get older. If at all humanly possible, do it. Make peace with your family.

I do a lot of work in the area of bioethics, and I go to a lot of meetings to continue to explore these issues. I have to make life-and-death decisions. In my role as a medical guardian, sometimes I have to make the decision to pull the plug. I have to make sure that I remain focused and balanced on these issues.

We had a young woman ... I don't know how old she was, she identified herself as 27 or 28 years old. The mother of a small child, she had been diagnosed with terminal cervical cancer. She was a member of the Christian Science religion and refused all traditional medical treatment. This was difficult for me. She was in hospice care almost dead and refusing treatment. She would not give us any information as to the location of her child or family. We were unsure of whether she was competent. To see if she was competent, the state stepped in and did an Involuntary Court-Ordered Treatment Process. She was deemed competent and allowed to go to a Christian Scientists' respite home. The person who brought her to the respite home became concerned about her welfare and brought her back to the hospital where she died. It was difficult for me to see a young woman that age make the decision to die. I had to remember that if she makes the decision as a competent, rational person, I have to respect that decision. When dealing with people as a guardian, I have to use "Substitute of Judgment." I have to think about what this person would want. This is why it is so important to have advance directives and tell somebody what you want.

I was close to my father, and it was the most traumatic event in my life when he died. I never thought that I would be strong enough to deal with other people's mortality and my own mortality. But I have learned that I can do this work. Everyone told me that upon the death of my father, his strength would be passed to me. It has. I took his strength and his courage. He always believed that I could make magic with people in their lives. He saw what I could do and encouraged me.

I still grow every day from this job. I can deal with life in a balanced way. I try to remember my goal and to keep focused on that goal. In the beginning, I wanted to save everybody: Suzy Social Worker wants to run in and save everybody. I have to remember that people have the right to determine how they want to live. If you are doing your job as a social worker, you are not making people's decisions. You are helping them to make decisions that are best for their lives and giving them the tools and knowledge and some of the information they need to make good decisions for themselves. That is really what social workers do. We don't make decisions for people. We help them to make positive decisions for themselves.

This isn't easy work. Right now, I am on leave from my job because of the stress of my work. My body has finally said that it's too much, so I'm taking leave for about 2 to 4 weeks. I'll probably be back before then. I need to be in there doing my job. There is no greater cause than to be dedicated to our families, children, and communities.

❖ HANNAH FREESE

For a long time, I heard the calling to social work, and I said, "I'm going to ignore it." It was like I could hear the phone ringing and did not pick it up. It all started when I was in high school. They had a thing called "interim week," where you do something outside of your curriculum for a week or two. I did an internship at a day care center. I worked with underprivileged kids, and it snowballed from there. Every project I did every year involved some type of social service with children.

When I graduated from high school, I was waiting tables and thinking, "What am I going to do with my life?" So I moved to L.A. because I wanted to act. I didn't want to do social work. I ended up with a job at a homeless shelter for runaway kids because I needed more money, and it was something I knew how to do. I realized when I got that job, though, that it wasn't just to pay the rent; I felt fulfilled. After almost a year, I decided to go back to Chicago and get into social work. I have a real affection for children, and every experience I have with children changes me. Everything that I've done since I was in high school has been with children. I've worked with Head Start. I've worked with runaway children. I've worked with children who were committed to the state.

I've had some intense experiences working with children in foster care. I was working with a family of four children—two brothers and two sisters. They all lived together and were all happy. Their father was in jail; nobody knew where their mom was. They had been taken from their aunt because she did not want to take care of them anymore. I found out later that the oldest girl had told the aunt that the aunt's 16-year-old son was raping the 5-year-old girl every night. So the aunt took the kids to the police station and dropped them off, and said, "I don't want them anymore." She didn't want her son to face criminal charges.

One day, the woman these children were staying with called me and said, "Come and get them right now." I tried to find places to keep them together, but I had to separate them. I had to pick the kids up—a 5-year-old girl, 7-year-old girl, 10-year-old boy, and 12-year-old boy—and take the two boys to one place and the two girls to another. I had to physically pull the 5-year-old girl off of her brother. I remember being on my way to get them, and I said to my supervisor, "You know, I am not comfortable with this. This is not going to be healthy and helpful for them." She said, "You are a social worker. This is your job. This is about social work, not about whether those kids are happy." And I went out and did it.

I've always regretted it because it changed their lives horrifically. I let that woman bully me into doing something that was not even humane. I had nightmares for weeks about that 5-year-old girl bawling her eyes out and kicking at the gravel on the street, trying to kick at me to stop me from pulling her from her brother—and him trying to be the little man. I once was their savior and after that … I stayed with the kids for a long time, and eventually we did get to a point where we were OK again, but the oldest boy never forgave me. I would take the girls to visit their dad in prison. They didn't want to go because they had been strip-searched there before, but I was court ordered to take them. I ended up placing the older girl with her grandma, but the agency wouldn't place the younger girl there because it was rumored that the older girl was making the younger girl touch her sexually. So we had to split them up, too. And so I worked with them long enough, basically, to destroy their entire family.

I've heard it from a lot of supervisors that it's not for you to be concerned about these things. It's for you to just do your job—get the paper work done and get through the day. Once, I worked at a shelter for women and their kids. We had an outside babysitter for the kids, so the moms could go to work or go to school. I went over there to pick up one of the kids in the middle of the day to take them to a doctor's appointment. I get over there and the sitter says, "I need you to take all the kids right now." I couldn't fit eight babies in my car, and she's demanding, "Go back and get the van, and come back right now. DCFS (Department of Child and Family Services, the state child protective services division) is here, and I'm overcrowded. Come back and get these kids, or they will take the kids to foster homes." I run screeching back with the van, and I get all the babies out. She sends a note the next day saying they can't come back. She was 25 kids over the limit. She's supposed to have 8 children; she had about 30 children. From that day on, when the women had to go to school or to work, the kids were staying at the shelter with the staff. Well, I'm told a week later that those kids had to be somewhere during the day besides in the shelter, because the agency was paying people overtime to come in early and watch those kids. I'm feeling, "Well, does it matter if their mom feels good about the day care provider? Does it matter if the child has a minute to get used to the new provider? Does any of that matter to the agency, or does it matter that they are paying overtime?" I was told that it mattered that they were paying overtime.

It's a horrible thing to say, but the stuff that doesn't kill you makes you stronger. Here's what I decided: The children needed a day care provider whether the agency wanted to pay the overtime or not. The kids couldn't just hang out by themselves. And if the moms wanted to go interview somebody five times before they let their child stay there all day with a stranger, then that's what was going to happen—whether my supervisor wanted it or not. They may live in a shelter, but they are mothers, and they had that right. The agency had to deal with it. I might get in trouble, I might get fired, but it would get dealt with the way it needed to get dealt with, not just the bottom-line dollar. I was going to do the right thing.

I got laid off from that job. But if you're doing what's right, you're going to be OK. Maybe you won't do it there, but it will work out in the end, as long as you follow what you know is right. As long as you follow your heart, as long as you follow your instinct. I understand the concept of being in business, but that's not what social work is about. Because if you're making $22,000 per year, you are not in it for the cash.

To be really honest—and I sound like the most unforgiving person in the world—I don't know how to put it or who to direct it at, but this work made me hate in a way that I didn't know I could. These kids' parents … they also have their own story. You have a kid being tortured and tied up in the back bathroom all year, and somebody finds out and saves him, and it turns out mom was tortured and beaten and dropped in a basement, turns out her dad was beaten. It's a cycle, and it's horrific, and it's made me judgmental towards humankind. There is a certain point in your life when you need to say,

I'm an adult, I'm the grownup now. If I need to seek help, I need to seek help. If I ended up getting pregnant when I was 16, and I didn't know what I was doing there for a couple of years, my mistake. I need to get help and then raise my child properly. I need to break the cycle.

I've seen things that human beings are capable of that no Stephen King movie could capture.

When I was doing foster care work, I got burned out. When I got laid off, it was the best thing that could have happened. I did it for a year and a half, and it was nonstop running, 7 days a week, 24 hours a day. I had a pager. The agency could call me at 3 o'clock in the morning to go pick a kid up from the police station. I'm never going to be able to stop doing social work, but right now, I've made a decision to get more education. I'm 26, and there are a lot of things I want to do—get married, have children, get a PhD. I've had to ask myself what I want more, and truthfully, I'm having a hard time staying away from the field. But this work will burn you out and will burn you out quickly. I let 6 months go, and I can't even get up in the morning because I'm exhausted physically, emotionally, and psychologically.

The thing that you have to understand when you are doing something like this is that you will go crazy, and you'll burn yourself out and drive yourself nuts if you let it all get to you. You'll be useless to yourself, to those kids, to everybody. It has been difficult for me because I'm open and emotional, but you have to find a way—when a kid is crying, clinging to their sibling and you have to rip them apart physically—to not burst into tears in their face. You have to be strong for them. You have to do it with your heart. If you don't have the heart, just leave those kids the hell alone. Because if you don't have what it takes to treat them with some human empathy and kindness and knowledge and information, then you should stay out of their way.

❖ JOSEFINA AHUMADA

My mom was a Chicana—a Mexican American woman. She was an herbalist, and I think if she had been born at a different time with different opportunities, she would have liked to go into health care. I remember helping transcribe books on herbs and their properties for her when I was in high school. People would come by the house, and she would always have something for your stomachache and something for your soul. Some of her aspirations and ambitions were transferred onto me, and I think this is where I got my original aspiration for being a social worker.

I developed a social conscience growing up in South Central L.A. My parents moved there in 1945 when it was a predominantly Polish community. They were integrating the community; the first Latinos were moving into the neighborhood, trying to get away from gang activities and oppressive police tactics. From the mid-'40s to the mid-'50s, the neighborhood changed radically and become predominantly African American and Latino. A lot of folks were looking for a nice place to live, but as minorities moved into neighborhoods, white flight occurred. The majority of folks would just move further west. The only thing that stopped them was the ocean.

One of my earlier memories of running into discrimination was going to the local library and being told, no, I couldn't get books out of the library. I was a real studious kid, at least I was reading all the time. I remember going home and telling my mom that I was not on the right side of the freeway to be in this library. I remember what an impression that made on me. As long as you were inside the neighborhood, it was sort of like a cocoon. I don't think that I was really that aware of oppressive things because I lived in a very secure environment with a loving family. One thing I realized when I went to high school—which never occurred to my parents and never occurred to me—is how we were trapped. Now, when I look back as an adult, I realize how trapped we were. I didn't know any social workers. I knew doctors. I knew nurses. That is something that I had been around as a kid. I didn't really know about social workers until my last year of high school when I came in contact with a Catholic order of nuns, the Sisters of Social Service. Then, I learned that social work and social workers were something real. When you look back at the late '50s and early '60s, social work was different. There were no school social workers. Caseworkers from DES (Department of Economic Security—the welfare agency) weren't quite as visible in the community as they are now. It was almost like a hidden profession, at least for someone growing up in the barrio. The professionals that you dealt with were police, doctors, nurses, and nuns.

I thought that perhaps I had a vocation to go into religious life. When I entered into the religious community, it never occurred to me that there would be any cultural differences. I always felt so uncomfortable because I would take classes in theology and the New Testament, and the other students were all Anglos. Although some students were friends, I felt uncomfortable; I felt that I always stuck out. Eventually, I ended up at California State University Northridge and it was there I fell in with a group of radical Chicanos. Afterwards, I became disconnected from the religious community.

You have to remember that this was the late '60s and early '70s, and Los Angeles was exploding. We had walkouts at the east side high schools. We had the Brown Berets, the Black Panthers, and it was a very radical time for a young Chicano. I thought I had a call to the religious life, but at the same time, it felt like maybe this was not the right place to be. What I always appreciated about those early years is that it really broadened my perspective of the world. It allowed me to come into contact with people that I never would have had contact with had I remained in the habit.

After I completed my degree in sociology and Chicano studies, I saw a sign that said, "UCLA School of Social Work recruiter to be on campus." I ended up pursuing my master's in social work and then decided to leave L.A. for a smaller town. I got a job at a behavioral health center during the mid-'70s. In the early '80s, out at Kino Hospital, we put together community treatment teams as an alternative to hospital treatment because we kept seeing clients on a revolving-door basis. They would be stabilized, leave the hospital, and then in a couple of weeks, they would be back. Our clients were not making it to the outpatient clinics. The severely mentally ill, chronically ill—for a variety of reasons—would not follow treatment and respond to the outreach provided. It required a systemic approach, a coordinated approach to reach out to folks. That is what our clinical teams were doing. They were helping to build bridges between the hospital and the clinics. So we developed these community case management programs and also developed the mobile care teams.

My career has been really filled with opportunities to do new things. In the late '80s, there was a real need to redesign the behavioral health system. A centralized case management team was formed. The county and state entered into an agreement to coordinate and consolidate public sector funds to bring mental health services to indigents. We chose to funnel part of those dollars through a centralized case management entity. I got to be a part of starting up that agency, which was very exciting. Over the years, my clinical focus was community care, helping to design a case management system for seriously mentally ill people. Currently, I'm the director of crisis services.

However, I do have plenty of discouragement. I don't want to bash managed care. There are some very positive things about managed care, but it's very client focused—to the exclusion of family. A lot of the programs that flourished in the '70s and '80s and part of the early '90s, I don't see flourishing now. Monies for early intervention and prevention or education or activities for family members or significant others just aren't there. We look at our program here at the crisis center and ask ourselves, "How do we make a family crisis center?" How do you provide services to nonregistered clients, because that's what family members are. They are not the identified client, but they are in just as much need, as a secondary client. Managed care hasn't recognized that population. Certainly, rehabilitation will not recognize it as a reimbursable service.

Not too long ago, there was a class action lawsuit against the state for inadequate care for a group of seriously mentally ill patients. That brought some reform to how clients were to be treated—for example, time lines for care, guidelines for creating and implementing treatment plans. The days of paternalistic approach to patients—the approach that "we know what is best for you, accept our treatment plan and sign here at the bottom"—those days are over. It's a collaborative effort between the provider and the client. Clients have certain rights, and that's brought a whole turnaround.

One of the side effects of these changes was that it made everything more legalistic. Once you start upgrading rules, then you have to become legalistic, and then people are legalistic with you, even the clients. "I have a right. It says so here in this book." Over time, you learn to work with the rules and regs and to not be defensive about it. Also it obligates clients to take responsibility for their own care, just because it says so in the book. It became a partnership. I saw how, over time, the system really went back and forth, clients went back and forth, sorting out what their rights were and also what they were responsible for. For me personally, it's been exciting to record this process, to see how this population's rights are being protected. I see a lot of resiliency on the part of clients.

I used to pose the question, "Is it ethical to work in the system or is it more ethical to leave the system?" It's a tough question. Social workers are dealing with that question all the time: "Do I remain here and continue to represent these really oppressive rules and regs and not give services to people who need them? Should I be part of this, or should I be outside the system?" It is a constant challenge for me. Obviously, I've chosen to stay all this time because I can never figure out an alternative. I think if I had figured out an alternative program, I wouldn't be here.

I went through the Watts riot in L.A. when I was 18 or 19. It had a tremendous impact upon me, really made me think about how you bring about change. You just burn down everything in sight, which is basically what happened. Our neighborhood got burned out. The police officer stops some guy and gives him a moving violation, and it's like one too many times where a cop beats up a black guy. The neighborhood exploded, and it was just like wildfire. Being an impressionable 19-year-old living through that, I asked myself, how do you bring about change? Do you bomb federal buildings? Or do you somehow work within the system? I could never bring myself to think about working outside the system. I was probably too afraid to do that. I think it requires a certain fanaticism. A certain, almost total focus, a "take no prisoners" kind of attitude. You totally do have to live outside society. That didn't seem very attractive to me. I might be that radical with a small"r" but not with a capital "R."

Even now, sometimes I get discouraged when I look around and see that it's almost like it was 25 years ago. It seems as if we reached the peaks, at least for me, in 1975 to 1989 or 1990. I've seen a lot of ground lost. Part of it is that the whole culture has lost ground in terms of affirmative action. I think there is an assumption that a lot of barriers have been broken down, that people have opportunities. Well, a small handful of people have had opportunities, but not whole populations. For every Josefina that graduated from UCLA, there were hundreds of Marias who didn't. They are still in South Central L.A., have had grandkids, and those grandkids are on crack, or in jail, or dead, killed in the street. True, a small sliver, a little tiny slip of folks got to be middle class, got to have educational opportunities. But most didn't.

It is pretty complex. I think the dilemma is that the face of social work has to be black and brown. It has to be Native American. It has to be Asian. It has to be, so clients can see someone with whom they identify. That is what gets to be tricky. I think the schools need to emphasize diversity and leadership. If they have people who are walking the walk and doing the work in the community, they have to reach out so that we can begin to bring people into the profession. Of course, at agency levels, agencies have to be committed.

I feel that I can do something for my little Pooh corner of the world, one student at a time. The reality is that it is the Anglo face that is caring for the mentally ill. That means that we have to share with all those wonderful Anglo students who are going to become social workers so that they are appreciative of diversity and have sensitivity and understanding. That initial attitude that I had of "I'm not going to teach anybody if I don't get minority students" was going about it the wrong way. The majority of social workers that are going to be working with minorities are Anglo. They are going to need to learn something about working with minorities, and who are they going to learn that from? That was all part of the decision to work inside the system. If you go outside of it, how do you have an impact?

There was one client I always remember who taught me about being alive and appreciating life. This guy was in his mid-50s, toothless, a Chicano, weatherbeaten, and experiencing chronic hallucinations. Somehow, he always seemed to manage. He was the most happy person. His happiness was not a function of his illness. He wasn't being hypomanic or grandiose or any of those things. He simply was a truly happy, very spiritual man, probably the most spiritual man I ever met. He had a way of being in the moment and appreciating the beauty of life around him.

There was one occasion when I thought he needed help in finding a place to live because he'd been kicked out one more time. He announces to me that he had found a place. In my own judgment, I was thinking, "How can this guy find a place?" That was the attitude I had. "What has this guy found?" It turned out to be this old broken down corpse of a motel. He was so excited. He found this place, and it was within his price range on social security. So we went in, and the place was falling apart. The ceiling was cracked and falling down. He had been a cook when he was a young guy, and he was showing me the stove that he was going to be cooking on. The jets were broken, and there was no way that anyone was going to cook on this. The place was a mess. But this was a mansion to him. I said, "Is this where you really want to be?" He said, "Yeah." "Well, I guess this is where you are going to be," and I started helping him with this stuff.

I was almost embarrassed to go back to my team and say that I just saw this person move into this rattrap. What kind of social worker would I be, doing that? It was important to him in terms of his autonomy, who he is. It was a location where there was some work for him. He was there for several months. All my work with him was that way. The message was: Don't look at the exterior, look at the intrinsic value of what's here. I learned a lot from him. I've learned not to judge clients or to assume you know what they need, or you may end up advocating for the wrong thing. It's not to excuse why the state does not appropriate dollars, but I think at a one-on-one level, we can truly inspire.

❖ JUDY BUSH

I work in a high-tech environment with state-of-the-art, cutting-edge technology. I work with adults in the cardiac intensive care unit. Most of the patients are elderly, medically complex patients who have a cardiac problem, a heart attack, heart surgery, or a vascular problem. I help them with discharge planning. I help to decide if they are going to be well enough to take care of themselves when they go home, or if not, who will be doing that: a family member, a spouse, home health care, a skilled nursing facility, rehab, or what.

At this time, the intensive care unit is the physical environment of my caseload. I've done a zillion other things. I'm in my ninth year here. I've been reevaluating my work recently. There have been some changes in my personal life, and I need work to be more satisfying than it has ever been before. And lo and behold, it is not measuring up.

It's not the work, it's the group of physicians and the mentality associated with their cardiac specialty. In light of that, I might enter into a discussion of social work in a medical setting. We are certainly the children here. This is the doctors' playground, and we are invited guests. We are the only professionals working here who are not medically trained. We are definitely an ancillary, secondary service.

Medical social work is a different animal. You need to be pretty aggressive, pretty verbal, and very bright. You need to know the system, whether it be a hospital, a university hospital, or a community hospital system. Direct social work interventions—interacting and dealing with the patient—is almost the smallest and easiest piece of the puzzle.

Some doctors in the hospital have a collaborative approach, and others have blinders on. They only see the body as parts, the patient as a diagnosis, and themselves as "the physician." They focus on what they need to accomplish in patient care and fail to recognize nonmedical problems as significant. I've been working with the ICU doctors for almost three 3 years now, and they can pass me in the hall without recognizing me. I mean, they know me … how could they miss me! I have to assume that they just ignore me.

To be a little more specific—and judgmental—the pediatric teams and family practice teams have a lot more heart. They seem to recognize that a patient with medical problems also has nonmedical problems. They take these problems into consideration and welcome social workers' involvement. On the other hand, the cardiologists and the cardiothoracic surgeons—the guys who do open-heart surgery—hardly recognize the impact of the diagnosis and treatment on the patient. They are doing surgeries on 65+, 75+ aged people and they fail to realize that major open-heart surgery might be a bit more traumatic for the patient.

I think this has to do with the nature of medical education. For MDs, there is no emphasis on the effect of treatment of a disease or healing from a disease on the family. There is a big chunk left out of their education. Their educational process overlooks or undervalues the psychosocial aspects of patient care. That is what we, as social workers, are trained to do. But if they do not recognize our value, then we are either treated as second-class citizens or we have to prove over and over again that we have something to offer that we can, in fact, help them in their practice and make their patients' recovery more comfortable.

Historically, hospitals included social work as part of their care. Initially, social workers provided counseling. Then of course, hospitals changed, social work changed, and there was less counseling. As hospital reimbursement changed in the early '80s, social work made a huge switch from counseling interventions to discharge planning. So now, to justify our employment, we have to say that we are valuable in saving the hospital money. That can only be measured in discharge planning activities. It is more difficult to demonstrate the value of counseling interventions.

There are very few managed-care programs that employ social workers. They provide for the patients' medial needs but not their social needs. Commercial HMOs will not pay for a patient's transportation to a medical facility. They will not pay for lodging for a medical treatment for out-of-town patients. They are very cut-and-dried as to what they consider medical, even if this attitude impedes the patients' getting to and benefiting from medical care. Based on my experience, I have a hardened point of view about managed care. HMOs and managed care either wait for you to die or get better. It is a business, and making money is the goal. As far as human beings are concerned, the co-mingling of health care and business is ugly and ineffective. It makes a few people very rich. That's all that matters.

There are good things about my job and good things about social work. I want to do the work that I was trained to do and the work that I know I do well and is in my heart and head. In medicine, I think you have to be tough. Personality is a very strong factor in the medical environment. Those poor medical students have to have a very thick skin and a strong stomach. They are grilled and humiliated in front of each other. It is a tough place, and it's not unusual that by the time the medical students become attending physicians, they are shut down to human needs. They had to shut themselves down to survive. Also, they are the crème de la crème in our society. They have to be the smartest and have the money, or know how to get it, to get into medical school. They are young and healthy. They don't know what it is to wear a medical gown and have their rear end hang out naked. They don't know what it's like to be stuck with needles or to be frightened by a diagnosis that hasn't been explained well.

I shudder to think what would happen here if there were no social workers. A coworker once said that we are the soul of the hospital. That may sound egotistical, but it is true. I feel that I bring a certain humanity to a patient's experience in the hospital. When patients are frightened and uninformed and have no idea what is happening, when they think that their life is at risk, I come in and demystify the experience a little. If I can do that each day, then I really feel like I've done a good job.

I remember a really nice Jewish couple. I'm Jewish, too, and we bonded. The wife was in for breast cancer, and it was a long hospital stay. She got really sick. The drugs made her crazy, and she was delirious, at the edge of her life. I spent a lot of time with her, and at the end, I realized that her husband was referring to me as her "chaplain." He didn't know what a social worker was, so that is how he saw me.

Now, I always go into a patient or family and explain what my role is because most people think a social worker is coming to see them only if they are poor or crazy. I mention that I see all the patients that come into the hospital, even though that is not really true, just so they don't feel they've been picked out because we think they are poor or crazy. I tell them that hospitalization can be a trying time, and I'm here to help them address some of the nonmedical issues associated with being in the hospital, be they emotional, financial, about what to do right now, or planning for when they go home. I also present myself as a liaison to a treatment team. Is the team answering all of their questions? Are the doctors seeing them enough? I try to empower them to feel free to ask questions. If they need a conference with a doctor, I can arrange it.

I was working with a bone marrow transplant team once, and our youngest patient at that time was a 14-year-old with non-Hodgkin's lymphoma. He had come in with his parents, brother, and grandmother. He was having trouble breathing, and he coded on the floor. There was a fast, smart nurse who called a code immediately. The team started coming together. I was with the family, and the medical people were doing the medical work. I had forged this relationship already with the family, which happens quickly in crisis, and that special bond and rapport allowed them to trust me. They were frightened to death, and I helped them through that nightmare. Fortunately, he survived that crisis.

That experience was good because I was part of a finely tuned group of people: a smart nurse, a good social worker, a chaplain who knew the family and prayed with them. Everyone did their parts, and it worked. I think of that kid a lot. He has since died, and towards the end of his treatment, his 42-year-old mother was diagnosed with lung cancer. I think of that family often.

In this environment, there are powerful emotional experiences all the time. Everyone gets saturated and numb to it, and that is the danger. You have to watch out for that. There have been many soul-shaking experiences. I think we should have a week off every 3 months so that we are rejuvenated and can go on. We need to replenish our souls, but we have no formal support. Informal support we get from our coworkers, and it is valuable and appreciated, but we don't have supervision. That is a "luxury" expense that has been cut.

The important value to keep in mind, here, is the right for individuals to make their own decisions, regardless of the professional and medical recommendations. That is really important in this institution where philosophy about living and dying is very personal and varies greatly from patient to patient and from doctor to doctor. Scientists and physicians are experts in their areas and can give recommendations and suggestions, but the patient is the final decision maker. I sometimes have to remind the team that people are allowed to make their own decisions, or different decisions, based on their diversity and culture.

We are living in the mainstream culture and this biases us. We have to recognize our biases and address them or work in a place where we are not confronted with them daily. So if you are considering medical social work, it's important to clarify your value system. How do you feel about IV-drug-abusing homeless people who stink and come in to the hospital for a meal? Do you want to kick them out, or do you want to feed them? You need to know how you stand so that you can choose how to function in this environment.

In this job, I definitely fulfill many roles. I feel like an educator. Sometimes, I feel like a travel agent. I feel like an anthropologist. When I'm journaling, I feel like a writer. And I love to be the "Momma," to kiss the patients, to praise them for doing well. I love hearing about their lives. I love this work.

4

A Personal Mission

❖ **KAREN VAN VUREN**

I've always been a social worker. It's just something that comes naturally. I could be with a total stranger and within 5 minutes know the "essence" of their lives. I simply love people. I guess that's just the way I am. I went back to school at age 47 because I had retired from a child care business and wondered, "What should I do next?" I never, ever intended to go on to graduate school and become a professional social worker, but the undergraduate program went so well, and I was determined I had nothing to lose. I applied and was accepted. It surprised me more than anybody.

It is now 5 years later. Recently, I spoke in a psychology class, and the professor asked me how I seem to have such joy and enthusiasm while working with very difficult situations (I investigate abuse, neglect, and exploitation of vulnerable adults). This may sound strange or rare, but I know that I am in the center of God's will for my life. He is my boss, and although I abide by and honor my daily supervisor, the real joy I have in doing social work comes from Him. He gives the power, strength, and joy. There is great reward in the work I do for Him.

I'm human, so there are times when I get really frustrated. I am working with a woman now who has taxed me to the limits—almost—but 99% of the time, I just love my work. What discourages me at times is the lack of interest and enthusiasm amongst my coworkers. There are very few who seem to enjoy their work, but maybe it's the "perks" that keep them coming back—insurance, security, annual leave. As far as I'm concerned, a social worker is someone who truly enjoys working with people, who has a genuine interest in others versus someone who simply does the job for the paycheck.

I'll tell you about a recent case. An elderly woman in her 80s called one of the social agencies in town to request help getting her weeds cut down. This sounds quite simple and basic. However, our agency was called to help out because the lady would not allow the people to come in her home to complete the paperwork. For our agency to accept a case, there must be some allegation of neglect, abuse, or exploitation. I was assigned the case, and on my initial visit, I sensed the woman might be embarrassed about her situation or fearful of what might be discovered. I literally put my foot in the front door so that the door could be open a few inches so we could talk. I spent time building a trust relationship with this lady over several weeks, primarily over the telephone. I also learned that our agency had had this case several times previously and that there was a daughter in her 50s in the home suspected of abusing her mother, especially emotionally. I stressed with my client that our agency tries to help senior adults and stayed away from negative words, like *vulnerable, abusive, mental problems,* et cetera.

One morning, I lined up volunteers to cut her weeds. I tried calling her several times for 3 days prior, but no one answered. This was unusual; she usually answered the phone. I did discover that sometimes her words to me on the phone were more guarded than at other times. I thought to myself, "I hope she didn't die." I met the volunteers at her property and knocked on her door to tell her that there were workers there who would be making noise with their equipment. There was no answer. I told the volunteers to begin cuttings the weeds, and I called 911 and asked for a welfare check. A sheriff arrived and walked to the back of the property. He then came to me and said the back door was not locked; he knocked, no one answered. He looked in and commented to me, "I don't know if there is somebody dead or alive in there, but I'm getting my gloves on and going in." He came out about

10 minutes later and said, "I still don't know if there is somebody dead or alive in there."

He then called the forensic unit. They came, and I entered the house with them. They took extensive pictures. The trash was piled 5 feet deep in the kitchen and the dining room. The occupants evidently would use something and just throw it down, never picking up their trash. It was unbelievable. Used toilet paper was piled high in the bathroom. Empty cartons and cans were all over the kitchen. One could barely locate the kitchen countertops. One had to walk on piles of trash to navigate from one room to another. I slipped a couple times. I couldn't help thinking about my client, who ambulated with a walker, trying to walk in her home! We did not locate my client. The hallway to the bedrooms and the bedrooms themselves had stuff piled as high as the bottom of a child's crib. The police officer and I found a small slip of paper by the front door on a piece of furniture. It was the phone number and name to a car rental place. I contacted them, and they confirmed that a car was rented by my client's daughter and was due back at 6 p.m. that day.

The next morning, the daughter was on the phone to me at 8 a.m. She wanted to know what had happened, as the lights were on in their home when they returned. She was upset. She stated that they did not need our services. I told her it was unsafe, unhealthy, and inappropriate for her mother to be living in that environment. We made arrangements to meet the following afternoon. I had the fire department, police, and other health and social service agencies present when we met at their property. Our agency does not have the right to remove adults from their homes unless there are some significant health and safety issues. My client was a diabetic, and when we met at 2 p.m., she had not yet been given her insulin by the daughter. The daughter explained that her mother needed to eat. I explained that I had located an adult care home where my client could stay for a few days until we determined how to proceed in getting the house livable again. The daughter and mother cooperated, although the daughter was reluctant initially. The case took amazing creative social work skills and the multidisciplinary approach was effective. It was discovered that the mother had a broken wrist—no wonder, trying to navigate walking over all that trash with a walker. The mother eventually lived with her granddaughter and never lived with her daughter again. The daughter had some mental health issues for which she received some treatment but then later became threatening toward her mother.

I've had several cases that are described as "abuse of 911" cases. One of them was a woman who was in the beginning stages of Alzheimer's disease. She and her husband were Holocaust survivors. This man gave his wife everything money could buy for 47 years, but the one thing that he couldn't giver her was a cure for her disease. When the dementia started to set in, she accused him of taking her creams and lotions. As it turned out, he found these things in her flowerpots and other unusual places. She would call 911 and report that he had hit her. On about the fifth call, she reported to the police that he had stabbed her with a letter opener. The police asked why there wasn't any blood and then realized that the problem was with her and suggested to the husband that she get some medical help as well as call our agency. The husband had never heard of Alzheimer's and did not know what was going on and thought she would get better. The next several months, my client was in and out of geriatric psych units and adult care facilities. She was sweet and kind to most people, except her husband. He was so attentive and caring toward her. It was sad to watch. The staff of one of the psych units felt that because she had gone through the trauma of the war and being locked up, being in the secure unit of a hospital was giving her flashbacks, a result of posttraumatic stress disorder. They wanted the husband, whose mind was perfectly clear, to leave their home and let her live there. I took a different stand. Even though she was my client, I believed that he was the one who should remain in their home, and she needed to be placed where there were professionals trained to work with her.

We ended up in court on this issue. The client decided she didn't want to be in the hospital or go any place else, and the hospital told her that by law, they could not keep her there. They also told her she could sign an AMA (against medial advice) paper. She signed the paper, and the hospital called me and said, "Now we have a real issue. What if she leaves here tomorrow at 4:00 p.m.?" I contacted an elder law attorney, and he called the courts to get an emergency hearing to determine whether my client needed a guardian. Her husband became her guardian. His provisions for her are par excellence, and it hurts to see her ask to go home on a consistent basis, but going home is not appropriate in this case. It is a sad story. Her husband has noted that surviving the concentration camps and running through the forests dodging bullets during the war was not as difficult as seeing his wife's health deteriorate ever so slowly before his eyes. He feels so helpless.

I'll describe one more case. She was young (54) and actively working. She was known throughout the area by virtue of what she did, as her job found her making contact with countless departments every day. She was diabetic and lived alone. She was not consistent with injecting herself properly with the insulin, and this time, a neighbor found her lying on the floor after she passed out.

I went to do a home visit and could not believe my eyes. The ceiling in the mobile home was falling in. The trash in the bedroom was from the floor to the ceiling. She had so much trash everywhere—food wrapping, used toilet paper, empty spray cans. The couch, which was her bed, was missing fabric, and I could see the metal springs. She had piles and piles of newspapers. I explained to her that her environment was contributing to the decline of her well-being and asked if she wanted to continue living like that. She said, "No, I don't, but I can't do anything about it." I spent the next several months locating appropriate housing for this lady and getting her back on her feet physically. Her mobile home was destroyed. Last week, I placed another lady in the same adult care home where this woman is now. I didn't recognize her. The caregiver is a woman who has eight grown children, a grandmother. The caregiver has my client walking every day. She is losing weight. Several of her medications have been eliminated. It is amazing to see the power of love and caring and its impact on an individual. It makes my job so rewarding.

Obviously, these are not the golden years for many older people. I think that the bulk of society is conditioned to take care of themselves and not get involved. That doesn't stop me. I focus on what I am called to do. It is such a job to me to see someone's life improve. For example, I went to see a 103-year-old man. He is living alone in his mobile home. He can't hear, and he can't cook. His 73-year-old daughter called us because she was wanting to hire some help, but he didn't want that. She is old herself and getting burned out on caring for her father, but he thought she could keep right on caring for him. He was living like he didn't have a dime, but he had plenty of money. When I approached him and methodically explained options to him, he hired an attendant to come in the home. His daughter just couldn't get him to understand, but sometimes, a neutral person can come in and make a difference. I just feel great joy to see an elder person's life get turned around. His sure did, and so did many others.

Being a professional social worker hasn't really changed my life, but working full time has changed my personal life. Full time for me is usually more than 40 hours a week on the job and then I still have so many outside private interests in life. At 55, life for me is full of challenges and rewards. Living is giving, and I love giving to those most vulnerable in our society: the elderly.

❖ KATHRYN NORGARD

Social work is a calling, a call to do something. There is restlessness inside of you, and you have this opportunity to deal with that restlessness. That restlessness has to do with injustice in the world, specifically the world of our community, of our state, of our nation.

I stumbled into the field. I didn't even know there was such a thing as social work when I was a kid. My family lived in the San Jose area of California. We weren't very rich, so in the summer, one of the things that I did was work in the fields with Mexican farm workers. As a kid, that seemed like a pretty glamorous way of life because you were moving around. The workers were family oriented, and they had this sense of culture. It wasn't until I was in high school that I realized that it wasn't such a glamorous lifestyle. These kids didn't go to school, and the families didn't have a permanent residence. It was my first awakening to how unjust things are in our world. Here I was, living in a housing development right next door to an orchard where there was a shack that housed an extended family of maybe three generations.

I knew then that I wanted somehow to be involved in making changes in some of the things that I was disturbed about, but I didn't even know there was such a thing as social work. I was taking a criminology class when I met a woman who was preparing for the master's program in social work. So I learned about social workers. I thought, "Well, gee, that sounds kind of great. Maybe that is the way that I do this." And now, I am one.

I've been involved in some important community changes in my town. Some of us realized that there was nothing in town for runaways. Kids ran away, and they'd just automatically be locked up in juvenile court. So we started a runaway shelter, and I think that was important because a lot of the kids who run away have been molested or have difficult family homes.

Then, the state hospital downsized and changed its focus, and people with mental illness were sent out on the streets. So a couple of us founded a program in the basement of a church that was run by volunteers. People with chronic mental illness could come in and have day treatment programs.

The other part of my life has been working in the area of criminal justice reform, specifically the abolition of the death penalty in Arizona and nationally. I call myself an abolitionist because the first abolition in this country was the abolition of slavery. For those of us who are now working for the abolition of the death penalty, the similarities to slavery are just remarkable. Slaves were not rich. There was certainly a racial bias in slavery. Slaves didn't have the same rights—human rights, legal rights—as other people. There are a lot of parallels, and there is no way the death penalty could be administered fairly and justly, even if you put aside the moral issues. That is why we call ourselves abolitionists because we really see it as the second abolition movement in the country.

I guess we will get to the personal part now. My son was convicted of murdering two people in 1991. He was sentenced to death. It turned my life upside down. I'm just now beginning to feel more balanced, and this is 7 years later. I guess I never thought I'd have social work become so personal. I've had a charmed life in a lot of ways. I was middle class, white, I was able to figure out a way to get through college, and I haven't had it like so many people that we work with who are our clients. I guess what has wedded me to the other side of humanity has been my son, John.

When we adopted John, we didn't really know anything about him, other than he was this really cute, charming, mixed-race 1-and-a-half-year-old. What we didn't know was what John was dealing with. Later, as we became more aware, I certainly gave thought to the fact that he had lived in a number of foster homes and had been shuffled around. I know how babies need consistency and need to attach to their parents or caregivers. He had problems from the get go. He had a hard time learning, and yet he was smart. He had a hard time telling the truth and a hard time not stealing. When kids are little and steal and lie, you can usually help them, but we couldn't do that with John.

We were pretty concerned and took him to counselors and psychologists for testing. He didn't fit into any category. They couldn't label him. He wasn't quite this, he wasn't quite that. He wasn't learning disabled, and he wasn't really oppositional. All the interventions were aimed at trying to change our family dynamics and to encourage him to behave differently. It wasn't until after he got the death sentence and I got diligent and found his family that we discovered that his mother had been a heavy drinker. He was later diagnosed with fetal alcohol syndrome as an adult. But all that time, looking back, he certainly had all the symptoms of fetal alcohol syndrome, except for mental retardation. It didn't occur to anyone, even though people knew he was adopted.

I didn't face this trauma very well. I was overwhelmed, and I was petrified and mortified. One of the things that has been hard for me as a social worker is that I just assumed that all social workers would be against the death penalty because being a social worker means bringing forth change. What was so sad to me was to learn that social workers aren't any different in understanding the death penalty and what this really means to us than the people on the street. Probably 60% to 70% of social workers are in favor of the death penalty. That was a hard thing. It was hard enough facing the real probability that John would get the death penalty. When I found myself in a group of colleagues, I'd be quietly reflecting, "Does she want to kill John? Does he want to kill John?" I got paranoid in my thinking. It's a weird thing to be in a community and know there are certain ones who want your child dead as a solution to this thing he has done. It wasn't easy at all. I considered all kinds of options of running away.

John's sentence was overturned last year, and he now has a life sentence, but the change in me is still there. Something shifted. What I learned about the death penalty is that it embodies every evil that we work on changing as social workers. It embodies racism at its worst. It doesn't matter that you kill but whom you kill. If the person who was killed is white, you are more likely to get the death penalty. It never fit with any kind of morality for me that it's OK for us to kill our citizens. I've been able, to some degree, to imagine what it would be like to have a family member killed or someone that I loved killed. I certainly can get to the other side of it and know how angry and vindictive I would feel. Hopefully, there would be something that would prevent me from carrying that out. That is what I'd like to believe our laws do—help us remain civilized.

There is always going to be killing. That is a historical truth. We are not able to abolish killing. So the question is, "What do we do when it happens? How do we behave in a less violent way as a response?" The death penalty is a violent solution to violence. It's the most violent. But what happens when there is a death penalty is that it creates more victims, a different kind of victim. You are told that a person you love is going to be killed and has no chance of getting away from it. It's not like your loving stops because this person has done a horrible thing. You wait it out, and you watch.

Death row is a systematic kind of torture of human beings on both sides of the walls. If the person who has been condemned is lucky enough to have someone who continues to love him or her and visits and keeps in touch, then both lives are touched and are bruised and battered by it because you watch the person live in conditions that are not even approaching human. You wait until the death warrant comes and then there are appeals, but ultimately, that person is strapped down and killed. The death certificate says "homicide" because that is what it is. So it's now another homicide and another set of victims, but it's a set of victims that few people have sympathy or empathy for.

It's easy to get focused on that person who was condemned and think of how glad we might be to be rid of him. I think about Jeffrey Dahmer or other people that do these bizarre crimes. Clearly, they are not whole. The death penalty is also like a purging. We purge ourselves of some of our failures, that part of our own shadows that we don't want to deal with. It's like a sacrifice for the part of us that we don't want to look at.

It's hard for me not to be judgmental, but you know, there are a lot of people in the United States who are only concerned about making a living. I'm not talking about people who are just surviving in the margins, I'm talking about the people in the middle who probably have excess. It's hard for me when I'm trying to motivate people to get involved—even in the simple things, like writing a post card. I really have to watch myself not to get judgmental. I guess I see through a different pair of glasses. I don't believe it's OK to be quiet when there are things about our society that are wrong and have to be changed.

❖ ALLEN CUNNINGHAM

My goal in life is to make a difference in at least one person's life in a positive way. I work for Children to Children, an organization that helps children deal with the death of someone close to them.

Recently, I was working with a mother who had an 8-year-old son and a 19-year-old son. Her husband had been in the Air Force and died suddenly of an accidental overdose of inhalant. When they came to Children to Children, the oldest son had to drive her here because she had just gotten out of the hospital, and she was not allowed to drive. She was in a major depression, on serious antidepressant drugs. She had a flat affect and cried almost continually for the first three or four times that she was here. Meanwhile, her younger son was in the kids' group. The son was doing a lot of work around his father's death. In the midst of all of this, the mother's sister died of AIDS, but I was able to watch her move out of the major depression that she was in. I was able to watch her move into being able to take control of her life. They were here about a year, and after they left, she went to college on a scholarship and got her degree. Watching the transformation from her coming in totally debilitated to being able to move out and make some achievements in her life and at the same time watch her son move through his grief process—those are the cases that stand out for me.

We always tell our parents that we encourage them to let the children let them know when it's time to leave the group. Parents say, "Well, how am I going to know?" We usually say that the kids will start acting a little different or want to do something else, but they'll let you know in their own way. We had this 4-year-old who was here because his father died. After about 6 months, his favorite uncle was shot in a drug-related incident. Well, this little guy was at Children to Children, and while he was here, he did some play with some of our medical stuff in our playroom each time he came. He was also real active in our volcano room. He had kind of a routine. He would go between the two rooms doing some things around being a doctor and making the volunteers die and get well and going in the volcano room and just punching on the punching bag. After about a year and a half, one morning at breakfast, he looked at his mom. He put his fingers a little bit apart, and he said, "You know, mom, I only have this much hurt left in my heart. I don't think we have to go to Children to Children anymore." His mom came to the next meeting saying, "You guys told me he would do this, but I didn't realize it." It isn't usually that dramatic. But for children to be able to say, "Yes, I'm done here," is an important part of the process.

We tell parents that children will often replay incidents in their life until it begins to make sense for them and give them some kind of control in their life. That is what our playroom does. It gives them control. We had a 9-year-old whose father had been murdered, and he would come in, and each time he went straight to the playroom. Week after week, he would come in and put on a hat and a suit coat and use one of the canes. He was a mean 89-year-old man. He told us, "I'm 89, and you get out of my way." He'd shake that stick at people and tell them what to do. One evening, he wore his hat out to the group, and his mom asked him about the hat. He told her what he did in the playroom. She asked him, "Why do you do that?" He said, "Because they have to listen to me." So for the time he was here—that 40 or 45 minutes—he had people that had to listen to him. That was a healing process for him when he otherwise felt so little control in his life.

Working with grief can be emotionally taxing. One of the things we do here is provide opportunities for what we call a pregroup and a postgroup for our volunteers. The pregroup provides an opportunity for them to get centered and deal with issues in their own life before the families come so when the families come, they can be fully present. Then, one of the most important things that we do after the families leave is provide another hour in which we meet again, to provide opportunities for the volunteers to talk about what has happened: to talk about things that have excited them, things that have touched them, things that have worried them, and to get support from each other about that. It is one of the most powerful things that we do. A lot of our volunteers who stay many years have said that that is one of the reasons that they are able to stay. Those of us who work here full-time take opportunities to do that with each other at staff meetings and in coordinator meetings. Personally, when I feel it being too much, I hide away in a science fiction fantasy for an hour during lunch, and it helps clear my mind.

We need patience with people. We sometimes want them to move at a pace faster than they are able. We get frustrated with them or we get frustrated with ourselves when we don't see the things we think we should. So patience with ourselves, first of all, and patience with others is important. There are those who don't want to help themselves, and we find ourselves beating our heads against a wall going, "If only they would," and realizing that that is my judgment of what they are doing and they may not be capable of doing that right now. And yet, there are some families who have been to Children to Children for a lot longer than I think they probably need to be here, and they are probably in the same place they were when they walked in the door the first day. Some of it is them being unwilling to look at what is going on and make a difference, and that is frustrating.

It can be a tough field. If you've had grief of your own, it's important that you be willing to work though that—if not at first, at least along the way. Because what the grief field will do for you is push every button you've ever had around grief and loss and sadness, and you are unable to be present for the person you are working with if you're so tied up in the whole personal loss stuff. I think it's real important that you be aware of losses that you have had. We always make our volunteers do a loss line. For some of them, that is the first time they have ever done that. It is a real eye-opening experience, but it also is the first step.

I've always tried to have a real positive view of humankind. Working in the social work field—especially when I worked with the homeless population—I think I've gotten a little harder in dealing with those who don't want to change. The homeless guys on the corner, that is a lifestyle that they've chosen for themselves. At one time in my life, I wanted to fix that for them and give them things to help them change. After working with the homeless, I know I have to allow people to make their choices, which is sometimes difficult for the codependent helper in me who wants to fix everybody. I think that is why people go into the field in the first place. It's hard to temper that.

This work has helped me interact differently with my own children, which has been a pleasant surprise for them. I would not classify myself as one of those star parents. You know all the rules, but when it comes to your own kids, they are sometimes hard to apply. But after being in the field and applying them so often with other people's children, it becomes sort of natural for me, and I find myself doing that with my own children. Additionally, one of the things that we do here is called "reflection." You know, we reflect what people say and what they do. It's not a judgment; it just lets that person know that you are really listening to them. My mother was put into a nursing home 3 years ago with Alzheimer's, and when I'm visiting her, I find myself reflecting with her. She responds to it like our little 3- and 4-year-olds do here in the building. It's interesting to watch that.

Well, for the last year and a half, the agency wanted me to be the executive director in addition to working with families in the program. I knew it wasn't what I wanted going in, and after the last year and half, I know even more it's not what I want to do. At my request, I'm getting back into working more in programs. That is where my love is, working either directly with the families or doing outreach in the community telling people about the work that we do. Those are the things that I love doing and the things I think I do much better than sitting at a desk and doing budgets. I've come back to my goal: direct service work with families, especially children—making a difference.

❖ DANELLE JOSEPH

I got involved in social work because of the things I saw my grandmother go through when I was small. My maternal grandmother was Native American. In the 1940s, in order to survive as a Native American, a person had to give up everything and become white—give up the dress, the customs, the way of life. As a child, I saw her struggling with that and the emotional pain that she went through in giving up her way of life. That's how Indian people were told that they would have to survive. In recent years, I've come to understand that she couldn't advocate for herself. That's why I'm in the field. I'm advocating for the stuff that went on back then, when I was 5 years old. That is the reason that I became a social worker, to advocate for my grandmother.

I grew up on a reservation in South Dakota. All the women worked. All the role models that I had were either teachers or nurses. My sister was a nurse, so I went into teaching. I found that as a teacher, I couldn't influence any of the social problems in the area where I was working. For instance, children would come to school with six or eight shirts on because they had slept out in vacant cars during the winter nights. People would be drinking at home, and the kids would have to run away to be safe. There was the little boy in kindergarten who had a bullet in his cheek. He had gotten in the way when there was an alcoholic fight at his house, and the bullet was lodged in his cheek.

At that time, there was a lot of Title 20 money around, and a lot of state social service agencies expanded. There were job openings for social workers. I applied for a job at a town where a lot of people didn't want to go because it was rural. But it was close to where I grew up, on my home reservation, and that was where I wanted to go. I got a job there and got a BSW (baccalaureate social work degree) equivalency with Title 20 money, working on the Crow/Crete Reservation in South Dakota in the mental health department. For the past 2 years, I've been working as the medical social worker for the Indian Health Service. The thing I find the most satisfying is that I can be a bridge between two worlds that don't understand each other, between the medical system and the families.

We have a higher incidence of alcoholism because of the grief the Indian people have gone through, the loss of culture, the loss of spiritualism. There's been a real strong recovery movement going on in Indian country in the past 10 years, so there are a lot of Indian people gaining sobriety. The tribal alcohol program has an intensive outpatient program called Traditions that's effective, but lack of transportation and the high level of poverty prevents a lot of people here from using it. We have a real big void in the area of adolescent chemical dependency treatment. But the AA groups are growing, and there's a larger number of people in recovery now than there was several years ago. The "Red Road to Recovery" program has a lot of the same concepts that the dominant culture uses in their alcohol treatment, but it says it in a way that's relevant to the experience that Indian people go through. Plus it has a lot more traditional spiritualism involved because there are lots of tribes that continue to use their traditional spiritual ways. That's really been a key in their recovery. One of the things that we use is burning sage and sweet grass. The reason that helps is that people grow up with this, and it brings back supportive memories. When people grow up with something, leave it, and then come back, it's comforting. It's a way of praying, a purification process.

I'll tell you a funny story about when I was working as a hospital social worker. There was a family meeting that was scheduled, and I knew that it was going to be difficult because there was going to be some conflict. So I burned some sage, but I didn't have a shell, so I put it in a Styrofoam cup. We prayed that all the people who were there that night would be healed. Eventually, the Styrofoam cup caught on fire, and of course it set off the fire alarm. This nurse came whipping down the hall, and you know how nurses can be. "Wra wra wra. What are you doing? You're never going to burn that stuff in our hospital again. Naanaanaanaa." I felt bad because they had to take all the patients out of their rooms and take them outside because they thought that it was a real fire. They hauled all these sick people outside. I felt bad all night long. The next morning, my sister who was a nurse at that hospital said, "This is good, you should do this every night 'cause all our patients got well, and they all went home. Even that man that was dying, he went home." Then, I thought back to what we had prayed for. We had prayed that all the people that were there that night be healed. And the spirits and the creator interpreted it that all the people in the building would be healed, and they were.

When people get back to their traditions in prayer to a higher power, good things happen. That's the key. It's hard for people here, though, because their native traditions were lost in the early 1600s, when the Franciscan priests came. People have lost a good part of their traditional spiritual ways, and it's been replaced with Catholicism. Some people are going back to sweats, and that's a traditional part of the O'odham Indian culture. There's a sweat lodge between here and the health department. A sweat lodge is like an Indian sauna used for healing. There's usually a sweat on Thursday and Friday nights for anybody who wants to go. That's been helping some people with their healing and sobriety.

I've seen a lot of people die of alcoholism. I went to a funeral last Saturday for a person who came through our detox program. She struggled with recovery, relapsed, and was murdered. She was 31 years old. She left three children. It's sad. But I've seen successes, too. One of the patients at the hospital was in a coma from alcohol-related complications. I don't remember his diagnosis, but he was dying from alcoholism. We were going to do an involuntary commitment to get him into a treatment center, and the doctor said, "Don't bother. He's probably not going to make it through the night." His family prayed and did some ceremonies for him, and the next day he became conscious. The judge came over to his hospital room to do the involuntary commitment and sent him off to a halfway house for 9 months. He sobered up and started working at some tribal jobs. Over the years, he progressed up the career ladder, and one day, I was at J.C. Penney's, and he was shopping for a suit. I said, "What are you doing? Getting a suit for the governor's inaugural?" He said, "I was elected to the council. I've come a long way in 7 years." Then, he shook my hand.

I believe that each person has a path that they have to go through, a plan that's set. It may not be a plan that the rest of the world thinks is good for that person, but each person has a plan that's put there by the creator, and they have something that they have to learn. That's why they're here. I sometimes come into their path for a short period of time—maybe to teach them something, maybe for them to teach me something. But I don't have any control or any right to try to influence what their life is. That's already been set. That has helped me accept some of the bad things that I see that are happening to people. 'Cause there's a reason for it. That doesn't mean that some bad things don't just happen. There are a lot of bad things that happen to people. I think it's our job to try to turn that into something good.

Seven months after my son died, somebody said to me that it would be good if you could turn this into something good. I freaked out. I thought how can you even tell me that this could ever be something good. His death was a sudden infant death. I thought about it, and after a year, I moved out of that town and went to graduate school in social work. I did research on grief. I received a fellowship from the SIDS Foundation, and interviewed 40 parents, parents who had experienced the death of a child, either from sudden infant death or some other kind of death. I found out that prenatal grief can go on for 14 years. We used to think that it went for a year. The interesting thing that I found out, that's been published in a small SIDS Foundation of California journal, is that the first year of grief, people are in shock and they don't feel the intensity of the emotion. The second year is the worst year, and unfortunately that is when society says, "Well, it's been a year, you should be over it, you should move on, get on with your life." The second year is when you experience the most intense feelings and have the most reactions. The third year, your feelings start to decrease until sometime between 10 and 14 years, when the person reaches their normal level of functioning.

A friend of my family, my brother's best friend, struggled with sobriety and recovery, and he was about 25 years old. He had been sober for quite a while and decided he was going to go on the Bigfoot ride. It's a horseback ride that follows the path of Chief Bigfoot and the Trail of Tears. It's part of healing the wounds from the past and a way of getting healthy and regaining sobriety. Anyway, he had decided to go on that Trail of Tears in South Dakota, starting December 29th. That's probably one of the colder times up there. Usually, it's below zero—sometimes, 40° below zero. People ride horses and camp out for about 30 miles. Just before the ride started, his cousin came and said, "Let's have a few beers," and they started partying. Somehow, they ended up in a car. There was a gun in the glove compartment, and they started playing Russian roulette. He was in a daze; he put the gun in his mouth, pulled the trigger, shot off the top of his head and died.

We went to a sweat a couple of nights later. The men were inside the sweat lodge, and another woman and I were outside. We heard this bridle clinking, and there were no horses there. She got scared and went back to the house, but I stayed, and his spirit talked to me. In the Indian world, if you hear spirits, it's OK. Anyway, his spirit said to me, "What happened?" I explained to him what I had heard had happened. He started crying. He said, "Tell my mother that I'm sorry and I love her." And then his spirit started to come towards me. You can't have someone's spirit touch you because it will make you sick or kill you. I said to him, "Stop and go into the sweat lodge where all the men are waiting for you." The others in the sweat lodge told me later that he did come in, and they prayed with him and sent him on to the spirit world. That was really, really, really sad because he had turned his life around. His mom was proud of him, and he was my brother's best friend. He relapsed because of social pressure. He didn't want to say no to his cousin, so he went out, drank to the point of being in a black-out, and killed himself. He didn't even know what had happened.

In my 25 years of social work, every problem that I've dealt with has had alcohol or other drugs at the bottom of it. It may not be the direct cause, but like children of alcoholics, the things they have gone through because they grew up in an alcoholic home. There's only one thing that helps overcome alcohol and drugs and that's people having a spiritual awakening and taking personal responsibility for their life. Just think; if everybody took personal responsibility, we wouldn't have any problems because we would all do what we needed to do to take care of ourselves. We wouldn't need social workers and counselors because everybody would do the right thing.

5

In Pursuit of Compassion

❖ **MARCY ALBERT**

There is no "average" day here. That's the way I love it. It is never the same. A lot of the job is crisis oriented. I've got a caseload of about 50 students. I work with kids ranging from elementary to high school. The youngest here is probably 5 and the oldest is 22. Because it is special ed, you can stay until your 22nd birthday. So it varies. I get the babies, and I get the high school kids, which is a nice balance. I get deaf kids and blind kids. I get kids who are mentally retarded and kids who are not mentally retarded, kids who are physically challenged and kids who are not physically challenged. That provides a lot of variety, too. I like exploring different issues. Sometimes, I am led down the road to juvenile court issues, and sometimes I'm led down the road to wheelchair issues and adaptive equipment needs. So I'm always learning. I've been at the School for the Deaf and Blind for 14 years, and I'll probably retire here.

Last Tuesday was the day from hell here. It was one crisis after another. The morning was spent getting an elementary deaf student committed into a mental health facility. He really needed to be there, but because of the system, he had to come here and fail again (which we knew he would) so we could send him back to the hospital. His mom was driving the car and he was kicking and screaming, and I was holding him down all the way to the hospital. That was so totally draining. Then, my afternoon was spent calling the police on a middle school deaf student who was physically attacking students and staff.

The thing that saved me was that at 1:45, my daughter was getting an award for excellence in a reading program. I got to leave the hospital and the police behind to go see another side of life. To see her get her award and be really proud and see the other kids at the school getting their awards put my life into perspective. If I didn't have that outlet right in the middle of that day, I probably would have gone home and eaten a quart of frozen yogurt. I think that it's hard to remember that life is not only hospitals and police. There is a whole other side, where people don't have to struggle to eat and kids are not getting arrested.

One specific student stands out in my mind as a good example of my work. She probably got here in about 5th or 6th grade and then she graduated 2 years ago. She was a Native American girl born with a congenital problem, which created very brittle bones for her. She was in a wheelchair, and one of her limbs bowed. Her legs were no longer than my arm, and they bowed under the wheelchair. Her arms were bowed, and one of them had actually taken the shape of the pad of the wheelchair she was in. She didn't have any range of motion. She couldn't bear any weight. She couldn't walk. Normally, when you pick someone up, you put your arms under their armpits and move them. Well, if you did that with her, you'd break every bone in her arms because of her brittle bones. She was deaf and bright. She was such a challenge to deal with physically that, as a team, we were always brainstorming how to find the best ways to dress her, shower her, toilet her, find her the best wheelchair.

When she first came to school, her physical prognosis was not good, not because of her brittle bones but because she was so open to getting pneumonia. She actually stayed in rather good health the whole time she was here. In some ways, I felt like her mom. Her mom and dad were wonderful folks, but they were far away. We would talk a lot on the phone, but I felt that I was the one finding out if she got her flu shot and when she last saw a doctor. I did a lot of the medical management. I felt really good when she stayed in such good health.

The team who worked with her were just phenomenal, especially the residential folks. I remember once she had this awful rash. She would always sweat a lot. If you were wearing a sweater, she'd be wearing shorts and short sleeves. Her body always ran hot. And there was no space between her neck and chest, where she had this awful rash. I just remember the love and the care that everybody showed in trying to figure out what to do with that rash. Someone came up with the idea to use a little bib, and one of the staff custom-made a little bib that fit under her neck that we could change frequently, to help keep her neck dry. That worked. But it took the whole team working together and brainstorming to do it. I don't ever remember hearing anybody complaining that she was so much work. They loved her, and a lot of that was because she was so much fun. She had a great sense of humor. She didn't have self-pity at all. Last I heard, she was doing really well on the reservation. We were able to get her a computer through the Easter Seals Corporation, and we sent that to her.

I remember another student who graduated about 3 years ago. She was sighted until about 2nd grade, when her vision started to go. She started school here in the 4th or 5th grade and was a day student because her parents lived in town. As a matter of fact, two of her sisters were already here because they are deaf, but she was visually impaired. Anyway, she didn't feel well one day and told her teacher. The teacher sent her home, and she ended up in the hospital the next day on a respirator. She went from partial vision to total blindness. She went from being ambulatory to being nonambulatory and losing all bladder control. We are talking about a really free-spirited, delightful young girl whose life changed overnight. I got involved at that point because there were all these issues to deal with. It turned out that she had a disease similar to MS, and it cycled up and down. She worked a lot with rehab, and she was able to come back and walk. For long distances, she uses a wheelchair, but for short distances she can walk. Her bladder control is just fine, and she has no problem with that now. But her vision never returned.

That all happened at the end of a school year, and she recovered over the summer. When school started, I really thought it was important for her to see a counselor because I couldn't imagine anyone going through this and not having issues. She didn't. She truly is the most positive, wonderful person I've ever known or will know. Her mom and her dad are Spanish speaking only, and she used to be but is now fluent in English and Spanish. She makes all the appointments for family members and serves as a translator for the family. She is incredible.

I keep in touch with her to this day. She is someone whom I've probably crossed the boundaries with. She got pregnant and got married, and I ended up going to all her OB/GYN appointments with her. Sometimes, her mom and I would both go to her appointments, and then the student would translate for me because I didn't speak Spanish. The mom knows some sign language from her other kids, so sometimes I would sign to the mom what was happening. I was there when she had her baby, and it was just so incredible. I still keep in touch with her, and I'll sometimes go to the doctor with her when she is having major problems. It's hard to be blind and not have the resources to go across town to get a referral. She is someone whom I feel that I have crossed the boundaries with, but she is always respectful of my privacy. She just deals with life as it comes and always looks on the positive side.

I just had to put a student back in the hospital this week. He's 9, he's deaf, he's probably mildly mentally retarded, and he has some mental illness. His language is very delayed. At this point, he can't put two signs together. He can sign "school," but he can't sign "go to school." You can't get anything from him about how he is feeling because he can't understand. You have to rely on what you are seeing and what his behavior is. It is heartbreaking. I know we are failing him right now and not even close to serving him well.

He's probably been here since he was about 6, and before that, he was in a preschool program that is operated by our agency. He's had problems since he was a little guy, and as he has gotten older, the problems have changed and gotten more severe. This is his third hospitalization this school year. The last time he was in school, he ended up biting the bus driver three times. He was released from the hospital, and when he came back, he never even made it back to the classroom before he was acting aggressively toward others and leaving campus. We had to restrain him and call the mental health people who put him back in the hospital. The hospital wasn't pleased to get him back because they had done everything that they could do, but he wasn't safe here or at home. His mom explained that he had hurt his grandma. I know the hospital is not therapeutic, but it's safe. We met the mental health folks yesterday, and they were going to meet with the hospital today. I'm trying to figure out where we are going to go now. Deafness really complicates things in getting him the services he needs.

It is so much harder to find services when you are deaf. When you are blind, they'll deal with you because the communication is still there, but when you're deaf, it is so hard. He pops into mind because we are trying to get all these systems to work together: our agency, the local school district, and the mental health people. It is still a struggle trying to find out where we are going to go with him. No one on his team has the attitude of, "Well, we don't do that." Everyone says, "Here are our challenges, and this is how our system works. How can we make these systems mesh together?" I'm feeling positive that something will come together, but it is a major struggle right now. As long as we keep moving ahead, I feel OK, and I can deal with it. As long as I see movement toward something, even if I don't know where we are going, I'm OK. I just know that we are going toward something, and we won't give up until we get there.

Another challenge we face is helping students make the transition from the school to the community. At the age of 14, we start working on transition plans with families, even though students can stay here until age 22. Those plans change a great deal over the years. It's very hard on a number of different levels. For example, the deaf kids here often go home to a community or a family that doesn't sign. It's incredible, the number of families that don't know sign language. They don't learn it, not at all. They tend to use lip reading, but the literature shows that even the best lip reader, and I mean someone who is really bright, only understands 60% from lip reading. It's just not a skill that can be taught to perfection. Some families know some basics in sign language but could never get in a really deep discussion about life. They can never ask, "How do you feel about that?" or "What are your thoughts for the future?"

For a variety of reasons, some kids opt to stay here. But the transition plan is really important for the kids who end up going home. Toward the end of their schooling, we try to work with the adult services, adult rehab, or the division of developmental disabilities in their home communities to get them involved. We try to set up meetings in their towns so the people in those agencies start "taking ownership" of the kids who are going back to their community. It's not unusual for us to get a call or two from agencies once our students are already transitioned out. We answer any questions that we can help them with.

I love being a social worker. I truly do. I can't think of another job that I would rather do. I could see being a social worker at a different place. I love this school, but I could also be happy working at a soup kitchen. I could do any type of agency work. Once I've retired from here, I can afford to do social work in a place that pays no money because I make a nice salary here. Most social workers don't, and I'm really blessed with that. So I figure I'll be here for a very long time, and then I can afford to volunteer.

❖ JOHNA REEVES

In the beginning, I had the idea that social work was helping people. For a lot of years, I used my energy toward what I thought was the helping process. I had a set agenda and helped people toward achieving the goals that came out of that agenda. My agenda was that people were going to come into something like middle-class values and lifestyles and get fixed. Something was wrong with them. A few years ago, I shifted. I now believe that social work is seizing opportunities that allow us to intervene and facilitate processes with people to help them make decisions. To do that, you must really listen, understand, and be informed about what's in the community so that you can plug people into what they say they need.

Casa Gloriosa and our journey of being involved with people who are HIV positive came out of personal need. My husband has AIDS. He was doing volunteer work and was asked by a gay man who worked at an agency in town to come down and give words of encouragement to sick men. Ken began going down there once or twice a week to read to the guys or just to be there with them. One day, our friend, who is now dead, said to Ken, "We like you coming, Ken, but it's my job to get people to test. Why don't you test?" They drew blood that day. When he got the information, he called me at work and said, "Could you come home?" I did, and when we read through the material they'd given him, we realized he had eight of the early warnings. So we just looked at each other and said, "Whoa. You have AIDS." Two weeks later, we went in to get his results, and sure enough, he was HIV positive. They told him he probably had about 5 years to live and that for the next couple of years, he really ought to do things he wanted.

Then, for the 2 years after that, expect to rest a lot. After that, he'd probably be dead. I tested, and I wasn't positive. Ken came from a history of being promiscuous and using drugs before he returned to his fundamental Christian roots.

The first year, we did a lot of sitting around and looking at each other. I realized that a phase of life really was ending. As we were trying to figure out how to deal with it, we decided that one of the areas where we saw a great need was in services for women and children who are HIV positive or living with AIDS in our county. Within weeks, we had an opportunity to help a woman whose child was dying. She was in prison, and her child was living with his grandma. This huge need was placed in our laps when we were not very equipped to do anything emotionally. We started moving around the community and found it was easy to get people to take care of this particular child. What we realized was that we, ourselves, had experienced a kind of sanctuary. This old grandma and mother in prison and the little boy who died had a wonderful sanctuary; and, probably, that model could be replicated in the community if we figured out how to get it started. We began talking with our friends, and that grew to forming Casa Gloriosa about 2 years ago. Casa Gloriosa is a residence for women and children where they can come and live. Now, we have 31 people living there, finding out about the disease and figuring out what they are going to do.

Our experience with that first family taught us a lot. Ken and I made up our minds to continue to speak for the truth as best we can. Once we talked through what that really meant, we found ourselves speaking in churches all over the city. In the first year, we talked to some 23 churches—very liberal churches and very fundamental churches, real big churches and little tiny churches. We started in the faith community because we saw it as fertile ground to respond to a community of people who were hurting so much from this disease. However, we soon realized that there is great prejudice and discrimination and ignorance about the disease. Ken comes from a very fundamental faith background and used that to say to the Christian community, "You say you want pitiful people. Well, here we are. You need to learn how to deal with us and how to make it safe." We began to challenge them: "How dare you have people coming in here, and you don't know who is among you? Look at us. We are people with the disease. How dare you allow your system called 'sanctuary' to be so unsafe? Let's talk about universal precautions." That was our entry into the faith community. Out of that, the faith community became responsive enough to buy a facility that now houses women and children.

The program follows my philosophy that you give unconditional care, but you can only do that when you don't have a specific agenda. Our goal is to serve women and kids who are HIV affected or infected. What is this service? I don't know until they tell me what they need. So there is an awful lot of listening. We've had people come there to live until they die and people everywhere in that continuum. Most of them live at Casa Gloriosa a few months and then go back into the community. We have support groups that run for months at a time and then that is not what the group needs any more. The children's program has evolved, and in the summer, we have a day program for 3 days a week. We should be looking at the potential and capability of kids and giving them good opportunities and energy.

We just try to listen to the client and—as long as it's ethical and legal—we try to respond. For example, we served a woman with three grandkids whose daughter was dying. They literally lived in two big cinderblock rooms. The first time I went to her house, she invited me into her living room, which was an open space with a lot of furniture. I realized as we talked that what she really needed was a roof and doors, windows, and electricity. We went back to some of the funding sources we have, presented her need, and a group of people went out and put a roof on. It might seem like a really little thing, but in the life of that family, it changed them forever.

One story is imprinted on my mind and spirit because it was my first experience being closely connected to someone who died from AIDS. Renee was 31 years old. She not only had AIDS and was dying, but she had had a stroke and was paralyzed. She was bedridden, and one of us took care of her day and night. Renee came from a family with a strong fundamental faith. Her mother and other Christian people visited her, prayed with her, read the Bible with her, and played music. That was the theme of her life. One night on my shift, she was very sick. I knew that she might need to be taken to the hospital or that she could even die that night. I was hypervigilant. Her room was a short distance from the living room where I was trying to sleep on the sofa. I had just dozed off when I was awakened by a noise. It wasn't words, it was music. I thought that one of the women had gotten up and turned on a radio, but it was 2:00 in the morning. It seemed like the music was coming from Renee's room. My first thought was that I wondered how she had managed to turn on the radio. I stepped into the room to see what was going on, and I saw Renee lying on her side with her eyes open. When I got close to her, she said, "The music, Johna. The music." I said yes, that the music had caused me to wake up. She reached up with her one hand and pulled me close to her. "No," she said, "the music is heaven." I searched everywhere to find where the music was coming from, but I could find nothing. I sat with her until about 5:30 that morning because this sound was just so precious. I don't know what it was, but I sat there holding Renee's hand and listening to her response to this sound that she perceived was from somewhere else, and it was wonderful.

The work of Casa Gloriosa is wonderful in that most of our clients are women who are just out of drug use or promiscuous lifestyles. You can see a change because they are sick. It's not necessarily a value change, but it's a pause in the type of behavior that has brought hurt to their children. Because they are so sick, they pause, and then what you see are these great exchanges between the moms and their kids. Some of them have said, "You know, Johna, if I get well tomorrow, I'll step back into using drugs." I tell them that today they are sick, so they ought to visit their kids.

There are three kids who ask me to go down on the Avenue about every 6 weeks to find their mother. Right now, she is in a nursing home, but if she gets well enough, she'll leave the nursing home and will be back down on the Avenue, shooting up heroin and laying her body down. But those beautiful boys, ages 7, 9, and 11 say to me, "Go get our mom. We want to see our mom." So I've learned her hideouts. I go down to where she hangs out and toot my horn. She knows who I am, and she comes out and gets in the vehicle, and I take her either to our home, ER, or detox, where she can get cleaned up for a couple of days so that she can have contact with her kids. I'm not trying to change her behavior. That's the difference. I don't have the energy, and I don't have the program, but I have three children asking me to find their mom so they can have some time with her. When their mom leaves again, I process that with them and try to help them develop some ability to cope with their situation and go on.

Many of our referrals come from doctors who want me to find their noncompliant patients and make them compliant. In the beginning, I tried to wrangle them into the house. I tried to get them into recovery programs. I don't do that anymore. I'm responsive when the social systems call, and I'll go try to find the person to bring them to see their doctor. The truth is that whether they take their meds or not is not my issue. If a person lives at Casa Gloriosa and they are on a medication, they sign a contract that says they've chosen to take this medication. When they begin to be noncompliant, all that I require is that they call their doctor and say, "I'm not being compliant." It's really been an issue of difference between Casa Gloriosa and other agencies who provide care for people with the disease. A person who has been given this death sentence has a rebelliousness, and using medication is his or her choice. Instead of using up energy on that issue, we just leave it alone. I ask, "What are you going to use your energy on?" For the women, that works really well because they usually will allow me to help them create time and space where they use their energy with their children.

I ask myself what I want to do with my husband Ken who, unless there is some huge miracle, will not live very many more years, and I ask myself why are we using so much energy toward all this work. Every month, I have a session with myself to see if I really am telling the truth or just living in a perception of the work. But it doesn't really matter because the fruit in our life seems to be OK.

I think it's important that social workers are really speaking what they are doing. It doesn't mean that we all have to have the same philosophy, but we should live what we say. It really doesn't matter what the clients are doing or not doing. Am I doing what I am saying? Am I living what I say is right and important?

❖ LORI SKOLNIK

When I was an undergraduate, I was doing an internship at child protective services, in the sexual abuse intake unit. I can't think of a particular situation, but I just knew at that time that this is what I wanted to do. I knew I was helping someone, somewhere. I had this feeling of purpose.

There is never enough time to do what you need to do in pediatric medical social work. It is very fast paced. Right now, my primary job is working with children who have cancer, but we are short staffed, and that seems to be the major obstacle of hospital social work as well. There is always more to do and so the other social worker works with all the other children on the floor, children with chronic illnesses and the abuse cases. There has been a barrage of abuse cases over the past 2 weeks, so I've had to fill in.

In this particular situation, I'm very conflicted because I don't want to see this baby removed from the mom. This baby has been here for a week, and I've seen interaction between the mom and the child. I've never seen anything more beautiful in terms of an interaction between a mother and a child and the bonding. Katie came in with a bilateral subhematoma, bleeding in the brain. The father was arrested, the mom denying that anything ever happened. I personally believe maybe the mom didn't witness what happened and that is why she adamantly denied that anything could have happened. But apparently, there was a witness saying that the father had slung this child—a 3-month-old baby—over his shoulder by the ankles and carried this baby upside down close to a mile, from a Circle K back to the apartment. This could have killed the baby. You know the mom did the appropriate thing by bringing the baby in right away when she noticed that something wasn't quite right. It is hard for me to deal with it right now. I see a very good relationship there, and the mom was just in a bad situation.

That's a big part of my job, assessing the factors behind a child's hospitalization. If a kid comes in and is malnourished, is it because there is a lack of bonding, is mom a first-time mom, does she not know how to feed this child? Does she not have the resources to feed this child? Is she not hooked up with the right community resources to be able to feed the child? Does she have a support system? So we evaluate the situation. On a pediatric floor, compared to the other social work positions here at the hospital, I think we do the most in terms of social assessment and evaluations in determining what the social setting is and how the social environment affects the child's health.

In the day and age of HMOs, the emphasis is to get a patient in, treat him as quickly as you can, and send him on his merry way, but there are other issues that may need to be addressed before a patient is discharged. For example, if a patient came in with asthma or RSV, which is a respiratory virus that is really common, they need to be sent home on a home nebulizer. The home nebulizer is a machine that contains a medication and helps the patient's breathing. Many times, we set these kids up with this home nebulizer and get them out the door. But has anyone gone into the room to assess what the home environment is like? Do they live on the Indian reservation, do they have running water? Do they have a wood-burning stove that is somehow contributing to their condition? Sometimes, kids are sent home on equipment like a nebulizer that needs to be plugged into the wall. But some people don't have electricity. You send these kids home, and you are really setting them up for failure. You send them home on this machine, and you teach them how to use it but then they fail to tell you or the nurse that they don't have electricity. Or maybe they are too embarrassed to admit that, and the social worker didn't have the time to go in and ask the appropriate questions.

I guess, in the day and age of trying to get patients in and out of the hospital as quickly as possible, we don't have the luxury of meeting with everyone and trying to determine if their home environment supports their medical discharge or if there is anything else that we could do to help them. But I try.

I introduce myself to families, and I tell them I'm a social worker here at the hospital. At first, people will freak out because they think that I'm going to take their children. They associate social workers with Child Protective Services a lot of the time. Or some people think you are there to evaluate their mental health. Anyway, it is a process of building rapport with people.

Some cases are hard to forget. There was a child, a 14-year-old girl who was diagnosed with acute leukemia. When a child is diagnosed with cancer and I have to tell the family, I will sit down with the family and the physician and the clinical nurse involved. We sit down together and explain to the family what the test results are and that the child has cancer. I really connected with this family. It was a great family, a nice family, and I can't tell you in what way we connected because we just did. She started her chemotherapy right away, and she was doing well, and as a matter of fact, 3-and-a-half weeks later, she was almost in remission. You can go into remission relatively quickly, but then you still have to stay on the chemotherapy for a 2-year regimen.

Anyway, she was almost in remission, and she came into the outpatient clinic for a regular appointment. Out of the blue, she had this seizure, and she coded. She had to be put into the intensive care unit and on life support. She was doing well, and then her blood pressure was all over the place, and her temperature would go up to 107° and then go down. She was having one seizure after another, and they couldn't find the source of the seizures. The next morning, I went in to see how she was doing, and she looked bad. The doctor who I was working with told me, "Lori, she is trying to die on us." I've seen a lot of kids who have died, and I've seen kids who looked like they should have died weeks ago. But this was so sudden. I mean, she walks into the clinic looking seemingly healthy, and, boom, she is in intensive care. She is still there. She has been there for 6 weeks now. She is not brain dead, but she is not responding. She is in a deep coma. She is not waking up.

The day that I came in following that attack, the nurses were all distraught, too. They said that they thought she might die because they couldn't find the source of the infection. We thought that she was going to die that night, and I just could not deal with that. On this job, you are expected to be the support to the doctors and the nurses and everyone else but then you have your own stuff to deal with. I came into my office, and I closed the door, and I could not stop crying. Even when I think about it, I start crying now. I just couldn't handle it. Like I said, I couldn't explain why, it was just a family that touched me and a girl that had touched me. The day before this happened, she told me that her friends keep calling her and feeling sorry for her, and she would tell them that she was not going to die. And now, she might die.

We don't have a lot of support here from the higher-ups. We use each other for support. This was a really, really hard case. It made me wonder why I continue doing this job. Not because I don't like it, but it is very hard sometimes. Emotionally, it can be draining. There have been many times that I thought, "Do I really want to be social worker?" I put a lot of energy into my work, and I am exhausted every day when I go home. The days that I don't want to be a social worker, I want to be a cashier—some mindless work! But I love what I do.

I like to think that I've helped people, that I was able to help them get through difficult issues. I helped them to be able to help themselves. I was able to give them the coping skills or the tools necessary to deal with life every day. If they could see that someone was there to show them how to deal with a stressful situation, maybe next time they come across a situation where there is a lot of stress or difficulty, they might remember how to handle it.

Right now, some of the social workers' jobs might be in jeopardy because the administration thinks that social workers can go, and they can put the nurse case manager in that position. I personally think they can do a lot of what we do because we do a lot of clinical things, also—clinical in terms of arranging discharges. I just think we have the training, and our training is valuable to keeping costs down in the hospital. I've calculated many times ways in which we've saved the hospital money in terms of the discharge planning and creative discharges and getting the patients out of the hospital. I feel that I don't take no for an answer, and I've encountered many people that won't dig further and try to get what they want or need for a patient.

I really believe that whether or not a person has the money to afford health care, I feel everybody deserves that right to be treated with dignity, whether it is in the hospital setting or anywhere. People come from all walks of life, and I try to treat people the way that I want to be treated. I know that sounds really corny and cliché, but I can have a really hectic, bad day, but I try not to show that. If I'm having a hard time, I can deal with that another time, but while I'm at work, people are treated with dignity.

❖ SOFIA AHMAD

My family is business oriented, money oriented, fast money. My family does not look upon social work as a prize occupation. It doesn't make money. But I've tried other occupations, and basically, I feel that the majority of my time should be spent helping people. Knowing that I've helped somebody who is underprivileged or the victim of domestic violence; knowing that I've succeeded in helping someone, knowing that I made a difference; if I know that I made a difference in this person's life today, that is what motivates me.

There are times that I know I've made a difference as a social worker. For example, working at the YMCA, there was this 12-year-old kid, Chris. The other counselors called him "one of the worst kids in the program." When you turn 12-and-a-half, they kick you out of the after-school program. Instead of having him kicked out of the program and having him on the streets, I asked him if he could volunteer for me.

One day, I was extremely busy, so I had all the kids sit in a circle and asked Chris to tell them a story. He says, "Once upon a time, there was a prince, who was a gorgeous prince, and his name was Chris." He goes on and is basically telling a horror story. "And then, there was this witch, and the witch's name was Sofia." Everyone started laughing, "Sofia is the witch. Sofia is the witch." Chris says, "No, no, no. This is the good witch." As soon as he said this, my heart just melted. He says, "She was the only witch that knew that he was a true prince and knew what talents he had." I had recognized his talents as an artist, and I always had him do art for me in class. It was a very touching moment. He was a kid off the street who would never show his emotions to anyone. That is how he showed me how he felt about me—through a funny story.

Another time, at a domestic violence shelter, I got a call from a victim. Her partner had slapped her across the face. He slapped her so hard, he ended up displacing her spine so far that it caused internal trauma. She didn't realize the extent of her injuries until 2 days later when she was in extreme pain. The injury gradually broke down her system because no spinal fluid would go through her spine. The spinal fluid leaked into her brain. Over a process of several months, she suffered neurological damage and slowly deteriorated. She called the women's counseling center, and I thought she was drunk or on drugs. Then, she told me what happened. It took forever for her to get through one sentence. She couldn't complete sentences. She would go from one thought to another. I spent about 4 hours with this woman on the phone until I could finally understand what we needed to work on. I went to court with her a few times and helped her prosecute her partner. I helped her get an order of protection against him. I advocated for her with hospitals, insurance companies, her apartment. She had no money because she was self-employed, and now she was unable to work and was out of business.

No one had the time to listen to her. But I worked with her for about a year. She is not completely recovered, but I'd say she is 75% better than when she originally called me. It's amazing to watch this woman and to think that she has come so far.

I now work for the victim witness unit with the state attorney's office. This work is discouraging. I want to advocate for clients and be more than just a paper pusher. I assist victims with obtaining an order of protection. We are the ones who spend the most time with the client. When I originally applied for the position, I was asked to advocate for the clients, to put the client in a shelter or to provide any type of assistance the client needed.

Now, due to the political atmosphere and a change of supervisors, my role is changing. To speed up the process, we have been asked to limit our services to clients. I was told by administration that the

victim witness unit workers are not advocates. I was told that we have
to separate ourselves from advocacy. If a client needs to go to a shelter,
then the shelter workers can provide advocacy. I told the administration
that I felt it was unethical for a client to leave my desk when I feel I am
capable of providing assistance.

I'm not happy with the administration or my coworkers, but I'm
happy with what I do, regardless of what they think I should do. There
are situations that have kept me going. There was one client who was
a victim of domestic violence who had a terrible experience with the
state's attorney's office. I keep thinking about her because there wasn't
anybody there for her. Every time I think of leaving this place, I think,
"What if another client comes in who needs help and doesn't get the
appropriate services?" I know that as a social worker, a human being,
a professional, I'm doing the right thing.

I've spent over 3 years doing this work. I ask questions all the time.
How is it that I can help the victim in such a small amount of time,
somehow convince her to seek help? How, as a society, can we stop
abuse? There are many programs and organizations that are focused on
the eradication of violence. Are they working? Where are we going?
Are we getting anywhere I may make a difference in a person's life
today, but how many more are out there that are not getting help?

I love to work with the clients. I love spending hours with the
women, but I realize that I probably can have more influence if I move
up and can help victims of domestic violence on a larger scale. I think
we need more people with social work values in administration to
advocate for these clients. I feel that I need to give up my work with
individuals so that I can help more people.

My previous supervisor had strong social work values. Being in
administration, she had an impact on the way we worked with clients
every single day. Now, with the change in administration, we have
somebody else, and those social work values are missing. That is what
I think needs to change in social work. We learn to work well with
individuals, but we need to look at the bigger picture. How can we
affect society?

I've had a lot of young people come up to me and say, "I'm thinking about going into social work." In them, I see myself. I was that
person at one time. I tell them that it's great, but you have to dedicate
your life to doing this work. And then I warn them about that dedication.
It's a good thing. It makes you feel great working with the clients and

helping people. But a lot of people aren't aware when they go into social work of what the consequences are. It's not a respectable occupation in society. People don't respect us. Politicians don't respect us. People don't want to give us any money. We don't make any money, and they have to be prepared for that. They have to learn to advocate for themselves, for what they do, and for what they believe in as professionals. Social work can burn you out, but when people appreciate you and you see the difference you are making—that is what keeps you going.

6

Building Community Connections

❖ WILLIAM LOFTQUIST

I have a strong interest in community change, rather than individual change, so I may not be the typical social worker. I use a community development approach to prevention work. The focus of my career has been exploring how local communities can become proactive and not just react to crisis situations.

Basically, for 25 years now, I've been working with local and statewide groups. We've become involved in a number of what have come to be called "statewide positive youth development initiatives." When people become concerned about symptomatic behavior—whatever that might be—these initiatives ask what the conditions are based on people's observations and experiences. What are the conditions under which these symptoms seem to occur, and what can communities do to take responsibility to change those conditions? From my point of view, that is basically what prevention and community development work is. We've published a lot of practical materials that give people a "framework" for community change that is fairly comprehensive. So that's what I've been about—engaging people in a community development approach to making their communities better places. They might start with a concern about substance abuse or delinquency. We've developed a broad, rather generic approach to community change that can be applied to any situation.

Our model has to do with the nature and the quality of interpersonal relationships. We call it "The Spectrum of Attitudes." It says that there are basically three ways that people view and treat other people: as objects, as recipients, or as resources. There is a qualitative difference between and among those three different ways of viewing and treating people. Much of social work, I think, tends to treat people as recipients. Through some of the consciousness raising that we've done, frequently, people come to an insight that social work and other helping processes may also be viewing and treating people as objects. This is not a very healthy culture or situation to maintain, particularly with youth development. I think young people serve as a metaphor for people of all ages. Adults who think they are in control need a major shift in their perspective from viewing young people as objects or recipients to respecting them as resources. That, to me, is the cutting edge of what is happening in youth work. We've seen some dramatic shifts from viewing young people as the beneficiaries of the good intentions of adults to engaging them and respecting them as resources and as people who have something to offer now.

One rather dramatic story took place last fall. We had done a successful leadership retreat at this school, bringing students, teachers, and different grades together. After a sporting event, an assistant principal was walking around the school. She came upon two rival gangs facing each other across the parking lot. Now, the leaders of these two rival gangs had participated in one of our retreats. They had actually been roommates and become friends during the retreat. When the assistant principal came upon these two gangs in the parking lot, she saw those two students, and they were handling the situation. One of them was going back and forth between the two gangs. She asked him what was going on, and he said, "That's alright Ms. Wayne. We've got things under control." She asked him, "Would you mind if I hang around a little bit?" He said, "No, of course not." She observed these two gang leaders providing the real leadership needed for defusing this situation.

Things are the way they are in most communities because of the way that people are thinking and behaving and maintaining patterns. That is culture. Some of these patterns of cultures are good and solid and positive. But culture is always a double-edged sword. There are negative patterns that are the downside of any culture. These patterns can be changed by being named and described by a variety of people who have looked at them from different vantage points and who experience them in different ways. If we want to understand delinquency, delinquent young people are some of the best resource people to describe the problem. If we want to change the schools, the students in the schools are the best change agents we could have. That is a big shift for many adults. Adults like to think they know what is good for young people, but that isn't always true. Their best intentions can have unintended, negative consequences.

A major role of social work is to create opportunities for people to look at changing negative cultural patterns, whether it's in a one-to-one helping relationship or in a community-building effort. For instance, when we are doing one-to-one treatment, more often than not, we see the burden for change as resting on the shoulders of the client. Even the name we use to describe the person almost implies the attitude that they are an object or recipient. It's very safe for the burden for change to be seen as resting on the shoulders of the person with the problem. In community development or in community problem solving, the whole question shifts dramatically. The question becomes "In order to bring about change in the circumstances which are contributing to the problems people have, on whose shoulders does the burden for change rest?" In this model, it rests on the shoulders of those people who are in the best position to exercise some responsibility for changing those conditions. The burden for change now might rest on the shoulders of the principal of the school because the principal is the one who has the most to offer through a variety of approaches: policy changes, practice changes, changes in the conditions under which students are going to school. This concept leads to very different strategies for change, strategies that bring about fundamental change through democratic approaches based upon respect for people.

Of course, it isn't all success. An experience on an Indian reservation in Northern Maine in the 1950s proved that. Our basic task was to help repair and build houses because, in that incredibly cold winter environment, the Indians were living in tar paper shacks. You could see daylight through the walls, and they had dirt floors. I don't know how they survived the winters. The community was segregated. The Indian community was on a point between two beautiful lakes, and several miles down the road there was this little bridge, and the white community was on the other side of this little creek. The Indians were not allowed in the white community after dark. That is how blatant the situation was. We were there for about 2 months, and the first Saturday night, we invited all the people in the Indian community to come up to the schoolhouse on the reservation where we were staying. There was a big field, and there were several people with musical instruments in our group, so we invited them for a get-together and played music and did square dancing and Virginia reels.

As the summer wore on, some of the townspeople began coming out to the reservation to the get-togethers, since there was no entertainment in the town. As that began to happen, the little Indian children and their parents would dress up more and more, and after about the first month, there was a difference in appearance of the get-together. White people were getting to know the Indians, and the appearance of the Indians had changed. As the end of the summer approached and it was time for us to leave, we decided to send a little delegation to the PTA in the local town to discuss how these get-togethers could be carried on, since everyone seemed to want them. The executive committee of the PTA decided that the last Saturday night we were there, the get-together would be in the gymnasium of the local high school. That had never happened before. That was a real shift in relationships and thinking.

One member of our group went up there a year or so later and learned that there was no follow-up. Nothing had happened. That shouldn't have surprised us too much, because the leadership was not there. The local leadership was not involved. There is something important to be learned from that. My definition of community development is that it is an active process of creating conditions that promote well-being. If we find that what we are doing helps to change negative cultural patterns and create those conditions, there is nothing that ensures that it will stay that way. We need to sustain, maintain, nurture, and continue the development because if that development process stops, it regresses.

I think there are some tremendous challenges to the field of social work now. I obviously have my biases about what I think would be a good direction to take. It's a dilemma because the job market is in one-to-one, reactive, individual problem-solving work. I'm not sure as stewards of shrinking resources that that is the best place for us to be putting so much of our emphasis. I would like to see social work be much more assertive and much more proactive in its methods and what it is about. Yet I frequently find that in a mixed group of people who might come to one of the workshops, it's not unusual for social workers to be the most resistant to this kind of change.

❖ GAIL GIBBONS

In our program, we work as a unit with other agencies. It's not "us" and "them." It's not the state and the agencies. It's just us. We are in this together. We administer the block grant that comes into the state to help supplement the refugee resettlement effort. There are three of us here. I'm the supervisor. We have an eligibility interviewer who takes care of the medical program, and we have a job service worker. We collaborate with several voluntary agencies in the community.

The program goal is to bring refugees into the state and assist them to become self-sufficient as quickly as possible. One of the wonderful things about the program is that it's a national and international network. It is very educational and keeps you alert to what is going on around the world. World news starts meaning something when the people you read about in the papers will arrive at your doorstep tomorrow. The process begins when a refugee arrives at the airport. They are met by a staff person from one of the local voluntary agencies and taken directly to an apartment. Following their arrival, we make sure that they have all of their medical needs taken care of. Many times, people coming in from places like Bosnia and countries of the former Soviet Union have tremendous medical and dental needs.

Within the first 30 to 90 days, they come to this office. The job service worker helps locate employment for them. There are some people who take a little bit longer, but most people are placed in a job within the first 4 months of arriving in the United States. Their children begin school, and the family becomes contributing, participatory members of our society. We have found that immediate job placement is most helpful for refugees. It gives them a sense of control over their lives. Coming from war-torn countries, most of them have lost control of their lives, and employment begins to give them back a feeling of power over their destiny.

The thing that I find myself becoming indignant about is the assumption that social workers are a group of "bleeding hearts." Sometimes, I think people view social workers as creating dependency. But no, we do not create dependency. We might give people a little help to start with, but the long-term goal is self-sufficiency. That is one of the things that working with refugee resettlement has taught me. People need a lot of help on day 1, but they sure don't need that much help on day 30.

The refugee resettlement process initiates with the United Nations High Commissioner of Refugees (UNHCR). The United Nations goes into a country and starts setting up safe camps for people to live. After a period of time, they have to determine whether or not a family can go back to their homeland. That is what distinguishes a refugee from an immigrant. A refugee is someone who is unable to return to their homeland for fear of being persecuted. Today, there is so much unrest, so much upheaval world wide, that not all refugees are given a chance to resettle in a third country. There are simply too many people to relocate.

Sometimes, one spouse faces the threat of persecution. Usually, the persecuted member will escape and live in a refugee camp and wait to be relocated. After being relocated, there is a process called *family reunification*, where the resettled family member can file an affidavit of relationship and ask for their wife, parents, or siblings to join them; it is quicker and easier. That is why single men are the first persons resettled. That takes time. I've known people waiting for 6, 10 years before a spouse can join them. Sometimes, families escape together, and the whole family requires resettlement.

One of my social work professors said that social workers touch the triumph of the human spirit. That is what refugee resettlement is all about. We touch the triumph of the human spirit. Refugees arrive in the U.S. somewhat dependent, but they are survivors, and 95% are independent within 6 months. They are out there as contributing citizens. Many of the social service agencies that I work with employ refugees who have been resettled.

Every refugee who comes here by definition suffers from post-traumatic stress disorder. Right now, we have no mental health programs to address this. We have tried in the past but have yet to find a workable solution. How do you provide mental health services to a population that, first of all, has a language barrier? In addition, many people come from countries where the concept of mental health or mental well-being is just totally foreign. They frequently come from countries where the family and neighborhood unit has been their primary source of support. Now, the very foundation of their life has been disturbed, and they have no social support. But trying to integrate mental health services into the refugee resettlement process is an ongoing struggle; it is one of the most heartbreaking elements of the work I do.

For example, cultural practices in the refugees' homelands often differ from ours with regards to domestic violence and child abuse. Things that are culturally acceptable in their country are not acceptable and even against the law here. We have learned that a lot of child abuse and domestic violence issues can be addressed with education. For instance, in one case, an older brother was responsible for his younger siblings while his parents worked. A form of punishment he used, that was accepted in their homeland, was to take the children and string them up by their feet. When we heard about it, we sent a caseworker into the home to educate the family by saying, "Look, this may have been acceptable in your homeland, but it is not acceptable here." Generally, this will work. It's harder with domestic violence issues. A lot of the women coming from some of the third-world countries are not aware that they have the right not to be abused. Education does not work with these husbands. Domestic violence in other countries is as difficult to deal with as domestic violence here in the United States.

We rely heavily on our caseworkers to educate us in the refugees' cultures. Not much has been written in this field. We have to rely on people's experiences. For example, there is a practice called "coining" that comes out of Southeast Asia. They believe they can relieve cold symptoms by rubbing a coin on the area of skin over the virus. When these children show up in school with marks on their foreheads and faces, the teachers often report the family to child protective services because of these unusual bruises. So we tell families, "If you coin your child and send them to school, the teacher is going to have to call CPS." Then, it is up to the parent to decide whether or not they are going to continue with the practice. This is a mild example of cultural differences. Some practices are more extreme. You may have heard of the controversy surrounding female circumcision. This practice is illegal here in the U.S. But in a lot of cities, the demand for this practice among refugee populations is so strong that people are performing female circumcision on the black market. Then you get into that debate: If they are going to do it anyway, what should our stand be? Should the U.S. try to make it safe and offer the procedure under sterile conditions? Or do we protect the child? I don't know.

What is really great about this job is that I get to see the resilience of the human spirit. I am amazed that often, people who are brought here and given the opportunity to take charge of their life again experience a healing process. Some refugees are the walking wounded. You know that they are in tremendous pain and yet they still survive. Refugees call themselves survivors. They learn how to make it.

My coworker, who I mentioned earlier, met his wife in the resettlement program. He was an interpreter for the U.S. government in Vietnam, and he would accompany troops into the backcountry to provide medical aid to village people isolated during the course of the war. After the U.S. left Vietnam, his name was discovered on one of the lists left behind. The communists began pursuing him, so he planned an escape with his younger brother. The only way to get out was by going to the shore, climbing onto a boat, rowing out to sea, and floating on the high seas. Some refugees floated on the high seas for months in very small boats.

The brothers were picked up after floating for days and days. Whichever ship picked up refugees became the country that was responsible for them. In time, even though ships would see these boats floating in the ocean, they would not pick them up. They would just leave them there because they didn't want to claim the refugees. My friend was eventually delivered to a refugee camp in Hong Kong, but they would not accept anymore people onto their shores. Instead, they placed people on holding barges. He told me that at one time, there were 900 people on this barge. There was little food and limited facilities for washing or using a toilet. They sat on the barge with nothing to do for 9 months with no end in sight.

Eventually, the brothers were transported here to the United States. My coworker went to school to be a typewriter repairman, which has come in handy in this office, because he can fix anything! He arrived in the U.S. in the early 1980s and was resettled by Catholic Community Services. He had been a teacher in Vietnam. His intellect and his spirit was such that within his first year of being resettled, he became a caseworker in the resettlement program and then worked with other refugees from Vietnam. He met his wife in the program.

Another gentleman I know was a psychiatrist in Vietnam. He was captured and placed in relocation camps off and on for a period of 6 or 7 years. He also became a caseworker at Catholic Services, and I work with him, too. His recovery has not been as complete as the first man's I described. Research has shown that refugees who had very high standing in their own country have more difficulty adjusting in the new country. Though he was a medical doctor in his own country, he could not expect to achieve that level here. It's not that it doesn't ever happen. He tried to go back to medical school, but after all those years of trauma at his age, he didn't have the inner strength. He said to me, "It's not just reviewing the medical material. You have to learn a new language, which means practically starting over." Some succeed at this; many others do not. But his wife and his two sons joined him from Vietnam about 10 years later. It took them that long to get here. His two boys are doing beautifully, now. They are both in medical school.

Although recovery doesn't always take place easily with the older refugees, we see a tremendous amount of resilience in the children. A lot of times, I say that this is why we do what we do. You see these little faces, and they don't have a clue what their parents have been through or why they came here. I love this job, and I'm going to keep it as long as it's here, until I retire.

❖ MARIA JUAN

I became a social worker because of a woman I met when I was a child. My father was a disabled veteran and spent probably the last 20 years of his life as a patient at the VA Medical Center. From about the age of about 8 until I was about 15, my mother's and my social life would be visiting him every Saturday and Sunday at the VA Hospital. There was a social worker there, and at the time I didn't know that's what she was. All I knew was that there was this real neat lady at the VA who whenever we went to visit my father was very kind to me and took me under her wing. She would show me around the hospital, give me paper to write stuff, crayons to color with, things like that, to distract me, entertain me, I guess, while my mother would visit with my father. I fell in love with this woman. I still remember her name: It was Ms. Beckner. She was always there for me. I started to have problems with my mother, and I would talk to her about these problems. She was my inspiration, and I guess I knew when I was 10 years old that this is what I wanted to do. I didn't know what she did or what she was, but this was what I wanted to do. I wanted to be a social worker. That's how I got started.

I work at the district schools, 2 days a week at an alternative middle school working with teenagers, and that is a challenge. I also work in three other elementary schools, and this year, I was assigned as a special education social worker. Most of my job includes writing developmental histories for the special education child study team. I interview the parents, and I report back to the team. I also do case management with the family. If they need housing advocacy or referrals to the clothing bank or to the food bank, I do that. When the community representative at the school is not available to get their needs met, then I will do it.

Before I got hired with the school district, I worked with domestic violence victims and people who were referred to me from the Tribal Court for DUIs or drug charges. My role was primarily as a counselor. So it was a change, but I really enjoy the kids. I think my heart lies with families, working with the total family—not just the kids but the parents, the grandparents. I see a lot of kids at the middle school and high school who are being raised by their grandparents. That is a trend that has to do with the parents getting addicted to drugs and alcohol, so these kids are being given to their grandparents to be raised. I have custody of my 3-and-a-half-year-old grandson, so I'm doing the same thing.

I think that as a social worker, I have impacted some of the families and the kids that I work with. Hopefully, I can influence them towards the right path in their life. With the high school kids, there is a lot of drug abuse and gang involvement. I get involved with the community, and I get people to come in and talk about drug abuse. I'm also involved in a real innovative program where we are going to start a sweat lodge for the kids. They can do sweats once a week to get rid of their anger and their negative thoughts. It's a purification ritual that Native Americans have, and I was lucky that my superior is letting me do this.

The sweat lodge is open to all the kids at the school. We have Native Americans, Hispanics, Anglos, black kids; it's even open to the teachers and the staff at the middle school. It's a purification ritual where they will be involved from the very beginning by collecting the rocks that they use to heat the sweat lodge and collecting the wood that is used for the fire. They will have a talking circle in the sweat lodge, and it will be like group therapy. It is a very spiritual program in that the kids somehow just open up and there is a lot of crying; therefore, a social worker or a counselor has to be there to process feelings. I think kids nowadays have gone a long ways from rituals. I've read that loss of rituals brings about the breakdown of the family, and then the kids get into gangs. So this will be a ritual for them, and hopefully we'll have other rituals later on.

Native Americans have one of the highest dropout rates of all the minorities. Every year, we have an award ceremony for Native kids who graduate. We give them a certificate to show that we are proud of them and give them a piece of Indian pottery. We include the parents in the ceremony. We do that every year. Slowly but surely, we are trying to get things changed, but I think a lot of it has to do with the families. Their expectations aren't high enough for their kids. They don't really push their kids, push them to excel. They just let them do as they please. The kids are dropping out because they don't understand the lessons, or maybe they are distracted because of all the problems around them. Maybe, it's the gangs. Maybe, it's the alcoholism in the home. Maybe, it's the drug abuse. For Native Americans, the family comes first, so kids will stay home if the mother is sick and there are siblings that have to be cared for.

I used to work at a high school, and I'd have teachers coming in and saying, "Talk to this kid, he won't talk in the classroom." Talking is not the only way that an Indian child communicates. Have him write a story or let him draw a story. Have him do something on the blackboard. A lot of our kids are visual learners. They won't talk, but they will communicate in other ways. A lot of our teachers are not trained in the differences in values of the Native American and non-Native. The time frame is longer. You'll see a non-Indian walking real fast, but the Indian walks slow. Native American kids could go to school for 5 years instead of 4 years because it takes them longer. That doesn't mean that they are incompetent or they are not learning, but it's just a longer process.

Our tribe is very much into education. The traditional people might be kind of leery of educated people, but they want the tribe to get ahead. They want their kids to succeed. A lot of the gaming royalties are going to education. There are something like over 100 individuals attending college from the gaming royalties. That's good because we need to get educated to get good jobs and succeed and to have a good life. You can work at McDonalds for $5 an hour, but you could be earning $18 an hour if you got your college degree. The kid whose mother is in college says, "I'm going to go there, and I don't have to be on welfare. I refuse to be on welfare." You don't have to be on welfare, you can go and have a job with some respect.

Sometimes, it seems like the whole family is involved in substance abuse. The grandfathers and their fathers, their mothers, their grandmothers are drinking, and then it carries into their children. Their children become teenage parents, and it's a cycle that has to be broken somehow. Now, we are getting into the harder drugs, like heroin and cocaine. I see that creeping in with the kids. I would say that most of our society is spiritually bankrupt, and the basis for recovery would be for people to get into spirituality—not going to church, but having a spiritual connection with someone outside of themselves, so they can show their children to be strong. So they can teach them to have that inner strength not to do drugs or alcohol and to have morals, character. I see a lot of parents who are just spiritually bankrupt, and they don't— teach their kids manners—"thank you," "please," and things like that are lacking in kids so often—and they are just wild.

I've always had a connection with a higher power, and I've always thought that families needed to be intact and together for the kids. Nowadays, there are too many divorces, and kids are the victims. It's easier for people to get divorced if one partner is not happy. They never talk about how it's going to affect the kids, it's just, "I'm unhappy, so I'm leaving. Goodbye." Then, they are with another mate, and the same thing is repeated. They need to have a connectedness to each other and a closeness and a commitment to their children and the community and their society. What they do affects their kids. How they live affects their kids. Most parents are just, "Oh well, my kids are drinking and drugging," but the parents are doing the same thing. Kids will do what you do. These parents have no clue that if they stop drinking, their kids might stop also. It's because they have their own problems that are so deep that they are hurting. That is the only way that they can anesthetize themselves to feel better about themselves.

I get angry at institutions, drug dealers, pushers, TV. I hate TV. I hate it with a passion. I'm sorry for saying that, but cable and MTV—I think it's such a negative influence on children. Maybe PBS has a few good programs. A lot of our kids are influenced by the media, and they are disrespecting their parents. They see that on TV. What's that Butthead thing? Terrible. I can't stand sitcoms. It's silly, and there is no purpose, and they say silly things to each other. What is the purpose? There is no education. It's just to laugh, and what are we teaching the kids? That life is just about laughing and that life isn't struggling? It's OK to struggle, and you can succeed, and you can be strong. Why should they always be laughing?

When I was young, we would all sit outside and talk to each other. That is what I see missing. The kids now say, "What did you do? You didn't have a TV? What in the world did you do?" I say, "We talked to each other. We communicated. We sang with each other." We tried to be together. That is what is missing nowadays with kids. We are all in this together, and we have to help each other.

❖ KAY STEVENSON

I had a commitment, and I pursued it. I started out in Louisiana working with DD (developmentally disabled) kids. When I moved out here, I went to work at the crisis nursery. I saw a lot of abused kids coming in, and I saw CPS workers coming in at all hours of the night bringing in kids. They had a real commitment, and I thought, "That is what I want to do." I interviewed for this position three times before they hired me. In the third interview, I said, "I can keep coming back as long as you ask me to because this is what I want to do." I've been here for over 10 years now.

I'm a child protective service unit supervisor for investigation. This job involves less client contact, which is something I really miss because I enjoy people. I enjoy the client contact. I enjoy the case management portion of social work. I have less of that now. What I have is keeping up with the personnel and trouble-shooting policy issues. I do get to work the more difficult cases, and I get to train new workers.

I've been able to move around a little bit in the agency and change positions. I started out in a general unit. Then, I was on a pilot project for sex abuse. Then, I came over here as a supervisor. I've moved around a little bit, and I think that has helped. I also do a lot of my own stress management. I don't take the job home. There are times when I take paperwork home because I can't avoid it, but I don't take my job stresses home. I run, I read, I do ceramics, and I do all sorts of arts and crafts. I've got a supportive family and husband, and I think those are some major factors in not burning out. I don't have a lot of stress-related physical issues. A lot of people develop some physical symptoms related to stress, and I feel lucky that hasn't happened to me. I have a Native American background; part of our tradition is walking in balance, and I really try to do that.

But I think my work takes away some of my family time. My children are grown, so it's not as big an issue as it was when they were younger. Fortunately, my husband is extremely tolerant. We can be at work at 5 o'clock, and no one's even noticed it's 5 o'clock. It could be 6 o'clock, and people are still working away. But you know it depends on me. I don't know anyone in this position within CPS that isn't so totally committed that they wind up working so hard that they don't even notice they are doing overtime. You need to get this done, and you do it. However, I think that I'm more committed to my family than I would have been prior to social work because I see a lot of dysfunctional families, and I really appreciate the family I've got.

There are certain images that you take home, and for me it's shaken babies. This really upsets me because they are such tiny babies, and by the time we get them, there is just nothing left there. They are vegetables. They can be blind and deaf and sometimes not even able to eat. It creates a lot of trauma in families. It's just devastating to see the effects of shaking on this baby that had so much potential. And then, we can't even find out who did it. Burns are also particularly bad. Burns are horribly painful, and it is difficult to see a child go through that much pain. I have an abiding faith in God, so I just put my faith in Him that everything is as it should be, and things will work out.

Working for child protective services is extremely challenging. The number of cases that come through is incredible. The demands put on my people are incredible. There have been times as a supervisor I think, "I can't do this"—not because of what I was going through, but what I was seeing my people go through and trying to help them dig out case after case and being hit with case after case. Some months, we filed more petitions then any other unit. To see my people buried like that was difficult. I have a real commitment to the people who work for me.

In investigations, we are right at that cutting point where families are in crisis, and we can turn it around and keep the children at home or we can take the kids out. If we can intervene and put in services and provide food boxes and get that family some furniture and suggest family prayers or some type of counseling or hook them up with outside services and somehow stabilize that family, that family can blossom. And once in a blue moon, we'll get a thank you, and that's all I need—once every 5 years.

It makes you appreciate what you have. Sometimes, I look at my neighbor's house, and I wonder what's going on in there. I think I'm more aware of the stresses the families are under in abuse situations than I would have been otherwise. I pick up on more cues and more warning signals than I would have as a lay person. That's good and bad. Sometimes, I'm in a grocery, and mom's yelling she's going to hit the kid. I'm going, "Oh, no. Not now. I do this at work. I don't want to do this at the grocery store." Usually, she doesn't. I haven't ever been in a situation where she actually did.

But sometimes, I wonder if it hasn't skewed my view of humanity a little, and I think it has. Especially in investigations, because I've gone into what would look like a normal family and found horrendous sexual and physical abuse going on. It makes me wonder, when I've investigated a case and go back a year later and do it again. I think, "How could I have missed that?" So it changes me.

Over the years, I've come to see that I don't have all the pieces. One of the things that I learned in sex abuse is there are certain windows of time that open up where a child is willing to tell about things. During those points in time, the child will tell you, and if you don't happen to hit one of those or come in an opportune moment, you could miss it, and the child is not going to tell you. I try to be really careful and do a complete, thorough investigation: talk to everyone, get all the evidence, get all the medical records. It takes more time that way, and we don't meet a lot of the current time lines, but when our cases are done and they pass my desk, I can sleep at night.

Human beings never operate on time lines, anyway. Case A is not like Case B, and sometimes we do need more time investigating a case. I would rather take that additional time and make sure children are safe. So I didn't do it within 21 or 30 days; I would rather say, "I did a good job."

I've seen social work go from more of a soft science, a people science, to more of a hard science, with an accent on quantifying and qualifying data. There is more paperwork across the board in social work. We have made a move from a people-oriented science to more of a behavioral science with objective data. I hate to lose the people component because I'm a real old-school social worker, but I also have a strong background in psychology because that was my undergrad focus. I did the lab—lab rats and all that good stuff—and I know that data moves you toward credibility in the scientific community, and I think we have that.

My people average a new case every day or every other day. We are supposed to close them within 21 days, but we don't always do that. It is intense. I've got a wonderful group of great people. They do it with a smile. When my unit is really busy, there is a lot of humor back there. You know, I've just got to smile and look the other way because that is the way they are diffusing their stress.

I've seen so many children come through. I've seen children battered and abused and sexually abused. You develop a commitment, and once in a while, you hear about one of your kids making that long haul down the road, and you know you've done something real positive. I had a kid come in one time and say, "You don't remember me, but I graduated, and I wanted to let you know." I had talked to him about things in high school. That did it for my once-every-5-years *thank you.* Just one child is all it takes.

I had one father who had 5 or 8, a large group of kids, and mom couldn't handle them, so he took custody of the kids, and mom was agreeable. Every year for 5 years, he called me and said, "This is really hard." He never asked me to take the children back but said, "This is really hard." We would talk awhile, and he would be fine; and he would call me again the next year. I work with another father in Texas who has custody of his daughter, and he calls me every year just to tell me they're doing well. It doesn't happen very often, but it's good to see they are doing well.

It's the most rewarding career I've ever been in. I love it. It doesn't pay anything. I didn't expect to get rich coming in, but I could not find a more rewarding career than child protective services. There is a passion behind social work that you don't get in any other career, and it's that passion and excitement that keeps me from burning out. I'll probably stay until I'm retired. I'm fairly close now. I'm going to retire when my husband does, which is in 4 years, so I'll probably bide my time. I do expect to work at least part-time doing social work. I want to keep my hands in it.

❖ LORETTA JAEGER

I grew up in another culture, the United Kingdom, which has a very definite class structure. There are the aristocrats, the middle class, and the working class. I came from the working class. Because I grew up after World War II, when the welfare state was in place, I received a lot of benefits. Our family had a safety net in place. For instance, there was a public health nurse who came to the house, brought vitamins, checked on the children. We had free orange juice for the babies and the children at a time when orange juice didn't exist for many. Medical care was free. Education was free. I went through graduate school with everything paid for by the state. When I came to this country where there isn't so much of a safety net, I realized the difference those social benefits made to my life. So I have a natural sympathy with working-class people, poor people, people who have not had many opportunities in life. The United States has been the richest country in the world for a long time, but we do not have a complete safety net for families. It's a patchwork with holes. It's frustrating to be a social worker here.

I'm a school social worker, and I think one area where the United States excels is in taking care of the needs of school children. We have a wide variety of disciplines which work together as a team, so if a child has a particular need, we have a variety of professionals who can get together to meet that need. Although we focus primarily on education, that covers a wide area of the child's life. It covers the child's need for speech therapy, physical therapy, improving the child's social skills. We have social workers who can reach out to the home and involve the parents. We have very caring special education teachers who work with the children daily and keep an eye out for the child. They are not just working on reading, but they are concerned with any kind of abuse or if the child seems sad. Some of my schools feed the children breakfast and lunch. We give them clothes. We give them Christmas presents. If they need dental work, we get them dentistry. "We" are the school psychologist, the social worker, the special ed teacher, and the school nurse. We together provide support to our children. This support is especially valuable to children from poor homes, although it's available to children from every home. Children from wealthy homes sometimes benefit from our services.

I'll give you an example of how the school is really a caring institution. We have a family with five children, and the oldest is only 7. There are

three preschoolers and two at school. The mother is from the hills of
Mexico. She comes from a rural place and is not sophisticated, not
educated, and is here with her five children. Her live-in boyfriend was
recently sent back to Mexico to prison. So she is now on her own. She
is in a neighborhood where there is a lot of drug involvement. There
were instances where people came into her home with guns and scared
her and the children. Last November, the mother quit talking. Until
then, we'd had good communication. She'd come to conferences. But
in November, with these neighborhood problems and with her
boyfriend going to prison, she quit communicating with the school.
She didn't answer the door, and she wouldn't have anything to do with
us. We discovered that she had quit talking completely, including to the
five children.

It became pretty clear that this lady was suffering from an
emotional crisis. From the doorway, we could see that the home was
becoming more and more disorganized, messy, dirty. So the whole
support system—myself, the school counselor and the community
representative—got geared up. We got together and thought about
how we could help this mother. This family was in crisis. Here was the
mother who was the sole person caring for the children, and she had
quit functioning. The kids were often absent from school, and when
they did come, they had obviously been neglected. They were dirty
and had lice. The community representative started to reach out to her.
Gradually, we have been able to get back into the house, and the
mother is starting to talk a little bit. The community representative
reached out by going into that house and cleaning it. It was awful. This
community representative and the health clerk at the school went
in and helped the mother clean up. And the principal, this is a male
principal, said, if you get all of the clothes and put them in a black bag,
I'll wash them. That's the kind of caring people we have in our schools.

Although it was frightening for her, gradually, the mother allowed
us to take her to a mental health clinic. She's not the kind of person
who would choose to go to a mental health clinic. But she has allowed
us to take her there, and she is starting to talk and to open up a little
bit. This is an example of how the network at school was able to help.
We are there to teach reading, writing, and arithmetic, but we were also
there to take care of that family's wounds. Picture what would happen
if nobody reached out to that woman. She's alone. What would happen
to those babies if she never talked to them anymore? So the school

system is really a little social service agency. The neat thing about it is we have access to all of the children in a way nobody else does. There is no other agency, no doctor, no social worker, no therapist, who knows all of the children, but we do because they all come to school. We see which kids are suffering, and we keep an eye on those children. That is why I like working at a school, because we have eyes and ears to listen and to watch the children.

Most of the families are receptive to our help, and we get some success. Of course, we don't always get 100% success. Here is a discouraging example. It was a family with four children and a mom and her boyfriend. They moved very frequently. In their lives, the children had been in about five or six different schools. They would move at least once during the school year and usually a couple of times. They ended up at my school. The presenting problems were poor progress—all three children were struggling with the basic skills, partly because of their lack of attendance. They were missing anywhere from 25 to 30% of all of the days that year. When they did come, they came late, and they would always miss reading. They were struggling.

It was my task to reach out to this mother. I was asked to get permission to test the oldest boy because he was struggling with his reading skills. We didn't know whether the cause was a learning disability or the frequent moves and the poor attendance. So I made some home visits. Several times, no one was home. One time, the boyfriend was home, and I stood on the doorstep and talked with him. From where I was standing, I could see the inside was dirty, messy, and very sparsely furnished. The boyfriend was willing to talk with me, and I turned on the charm. It's a social work technique to turn on the charm and let people know that you are an OK person and you can be trusted. I told him I needed some papers signed and left the papers with him. The mother wouldn't return the paperwork. I went back first thing in the morning because I figured she would be there. The boyfriend was there, and he opened the door and I said, "I just want to have a quick word with the mother to see if she can sign the papers so the child can be tested." He told me that she was in bed, but he would get her up. He went, and I waited for about 10 minutes on the doorstep. When she came out, she was so angry, so rude, so nasty that I decided I would turn the charm index up, and I apologized. I was so sweet. I was so nice. I was determined she was going to find nothing in me to object to because I was sorry I had gotten her out of bed, and all I wanted to do was to set up an appointment. "Could we please set up an appointment?" So that was all that we did. We made an appointment.

She didn't come. She didn't show up. After several efforts, I finally get her in, and I decide that this time, I'm going to win her over. I'm going to get her to see if we can just work together to get her children to school regularly and on time to help them reach their potential. I decided that this interview is my big chance. Well, she sat there with a paperclip opened up and worked on her nails the whole time in a very compulsive, stressful manner. She never smiled. I tried everything to get her to warm up to me, but she didn't. She continued to be rude, unfriendly, and blaming the school for the children's problems. She claimed we had not taught them. She explained that the reason for the kids' poor attendance was that she was working a shift from 10 p.m. to about 3 a.m. At 10 p.m., she would take her four children, aged 5 through 9, to a relative and put them to bed. Then at 3 o'clock, she would finish her job and pick up her children and take them home and put them back to bed. School starts at 9, and she would still be sleeping, and the kids, having had their sleep disrupted in the middle of the night, couldn't wake up to get themselves ready for school. She angrily says to me, "I'm doing my best to put food on the table, and you're telling me that I'm not getting my kids to school? I'm doing the best that I can, and you're not helping me a bit by complaining about this attendance." She wouldn't discuss it with me, wouldn't even open up to discuss any alternatives. That was very frustrating. I really tried my best to get that mom to open up and to work with us. I never even got a smile out of her. She went away. She pulled the children out of school and moved. They were evicted again. I recently received a phone call from the new school. The same problems—the kids are missing school, still late, and they still can't get the mother in to discuss special education for the children.

Fortunately, not every case is so difficult. There are many small successes every day. A child's behavior improves. A child opens up and shares, and you can help with some little worry or problem. Not all of the problems are big. Plus working with children is fun. When you work with children, you don't have to be that serious. You can fool around and laugh and joke. You can play games. You can be a kid. If you are working with adults, you might feel that you always have to be correct. You might have to be rather serious, and you certainly would have to avoid making mistakes. When you work with kids, they don't notice when you make mistakes. Every social worker is going to have a bad day when maybe you are not feeling well or you feel that you are not doing a very good job, but the little children still think you're great. You get a lot of positive feedback from the children. We give out a lot of hugs to children who are sad or need some nurturing. It is not always a physical hug, sometimes it's a pat on the back, a smile, or a word of encouragement, and sometimes it's a real hug. It's kind of neat to go to work and dish out hugs.

What helps with the burnout in my job is the vacations. When you have the summer off, it is rejuvenating. Yet even in spite of the vacations, I detect in myself signs of cynicism. You can become so rooted in the reality of all the day-to-day nitty-gritty and bad things that you see that you can start to develop this cynicism. I see that in myself. But I still think my job's rewarding because most of the time, we have some success with children. We improve school behavior, or help a child to feel better, or help a child with something that is hurting. It's all meaningful when you can have some success every day.

7

A Healing Journey

❖ **PAT BETARD**

I am a recovering alcoholic. I just celebrated 15 years of sobriety. My father died of alcoholism. He was 76 years old. He really admired my recovery and had an enormous amount of respect for it. He got to AA just a few years ago, and he and I ended up having a wonderful relationship for the last 5 years of his life. I will be forever grateful for this. Here is a person who is a late-stage alcoholic in his 70s really pursuing getting sober and really wanting it, even though he did not have a lot of skills and gifts. This is what told me that it is never too late, to not ever give up.

When I was growing up in Philadelphia in the '50s and early '60s, young women did one of three things: They got married, stayed home and took care of their parents, or went into convents. I was in the convent when I was 22. I didn't know I was a lesbian then. I didn't know that I was a lesbian until I was 40, and I'm 51 now. I wasn't interested in getting married, I knew that much. There was all this chaos in my home. I grew up in an extremely dysfunctional family, with physical, sexual, and emotional abuse. For me, becoming a nun was a way to get out of there. But I wasn't successful. It ended up that the convent asked me to leave after about 9 months. My sister attempted suicide for the third time while I was in the convent. A priest, who was a friend of the family, came out to the mother house and told me that it was all my fault, that I was selfish, that I should be home taking care of my family instead of following my own selfish desires. That just tore me up. I was hysterical that day. I got called to see the supervisor, and she told me that I should call my mother and have her come get me the next day. After leaving the convent, I spent most of my life being a secretary.

I did a lot of drinking in those years. I learned so much when I got sober in 1981. I thought that I would just get sober. It's good that no one told me what I was going to have to go through in life. I have done a lot of therapy on family-of-origin issues, relationship issues, and everything else over the years. I have done a lot of my own work, and there is a phrase that "the curse becomes the blessing" from a book called the *Wounded Healer*. That is how I think of myself now—as a wounded healer.

After I got sober, I went to Seattle University. I had worked at the University of Washington for 11-and-a-half years, so I had a little retirement money there. I took it all out and went to school. I was about 35 and so grateful to have the opportunity to go to school. The one area that touches me at a very deep core level is when I am dealing with a woman who is maybe in her 30s, still an alcoholic or an addict, and is losing her home or going to lose her kids. I see the price she is paying for that addiction. That touches me because my philosophy from early in my recovery process was, "There but for the grace of God go I." I came very close to losing a job and losing my apartment. I was single at the time; I could have been out on the street in just a bat of the eye. I have a very strong identification with women who are out on the street or on their way there. I feel a real calling, a responsibility to be present.

What was great about going to the Seattle University addiction studies program was their philosophy: Alcoholics can die very nicely out there without your help, thank you very much. Do your own work, and be prepared to love the alcoholic. If you can't do those two things, get the hell out of the field now—save your time and money. They do not need you. I am a sort of a black belt in Al-Anon, so I don't rescue people anymore. One of my favorite lines is that if you're working harder than your client, then there is something wrong. But within that, I will be persistent in giving clients every opportunity to rise to the occasion because somebody gave me that chance.

I have a very challenging job at the moment. I am the substance abuse outreach counselor in a public housing community. When I went there, I thought that I would be bringing individuals, couples, and families to my office and doing work with them. I set up my office. I had a little children's corner and the whole bit. I would be an old lady with white hair if I had waited for clients to show up. Now, I spend very little time in my office and have gone to much more of a combination of crisis intervention and case management. I do most of my work either in a client's home or in my car when I am driving them to appointments. Clients need transportation, and I want the opportunity to intervene with them. Unfortunately, many people are not able to respond to my offer of help, but I keep going back and back and back and back. I will do that probably four or five times. If I can't get them engaged, if I can't get them to do anything, then I have to let them go. I'll let them know that I'm there and that I'm glad to work with them at such time as I can be of assistance. At that point, the ball is in their court.

I find, with rare exception that I am able to gain a level of trust with clients pretty quickly. I don't make them guess at whether or not their intuition is telling them to do the right thing. I'll say very early in my first encounter with somebody,

> You may not always like what I have to say, but the good thing is that you'll never have to guess what I am thinking. If I have a thought, you will hear it. I will never play games with you. I'll never bullshit you. I'm a "what you see is what you get" kind of person.

I find that that is really critical because most of the people that I work with have been screwed by the system, have said things that have been used against them. They have, with very good reason, a strong distrust of professional therapists and people in the system.

I'll describe a client who recently presented some of the most challenging work I've done: single mom, 35 years old, 3-and-a-half-year-old son. They have been homeless their whole life; this is their first apartment. She's very happy to be there, but the money still keeps going into her arm as heroin. When I went there to talk with her, the little boy—there's an enormous amount of chaos with children in this community so I've seen children in all kinds of situations—but this particular little boy was the most out-of-control child I had ever met. We literally could not get him to stop climbing up his mother's legs and screaming and acting out for me to have even 1 minute of conversation with her. I kept watching the dynamics because she kept reacting to him in exactly the same tone that he was coming from. I had two really out-of-control individuals in front of me. I kept trying to interact with him. Finally, I guess he got comfortable enough to come within arm's reach of me. Meanwhile, as I'm trying to engage him, I'm thinking, "What am I going to do if he ever does get close enough for me to be able to grab him?" And I remembered this training I had gone through about how to care for drug-addicted babies. You were supposed to wrap the child in a cloth to reduce the stimulation. I thought, "Well what the heck, I've got nothing to lose. I'm going to try a variation on that theme with him." When he did come close enough for me to give him a hug, I kept my arms around him, and we walked over to a sofa that was in the living room. Of course, he's screaming and flailing. I'm holding him firmly but not tightly, and I realized that intuitively, he was trying to convince me he was a bad kid. The whole time that I'm holding him, I'm saying, "You know, you are such a great kid. I can't believe your mamma is so lucky," and blah blah blah blah. I told him, "I know that you have it within you to be quiet for 10 minutes so I can talk with your mamma. I just know that because you're a smart little guy." I kept doing these positive affirmations—nothing but positive affirmations. We were on the sofa; I just kept holding him; his crying stopped, and he started to relax. It took only about 5 to 10 minutes, but it seemed like forever. Then finally, he walked to his bed and lay down and started talking to himself. I finally got the 10 minutes I needed to do a mini intervention with his mom to find out what was going on.

The child usually spent his days at a day care center designed for abused and homeless kids. She said that the next morning, she had a doctor's appointment and no transportation to get there. She had dropped out of the methadone clinic that she was supposed to be in, so there was no bus transportation to get him to the day care center. It was too far out of their area. I agreed to come and pick them up and take him to the day care center. Then, I would take her to her doctor's appointment, which was a long distance to travel. I would have my first real counseling session with her at that time. It turned out that the teachers at the day care center were having a training day, and they couldn't take him. The three of us ended up spending the entire day together. The woman had never followed through on anything. She was probably going to lose her home; she was on her way to eviction, which meant that she was going to be barred from public housing for 3 years.

I spent about 20 hours with her over the course of about 2 weeks, and I couldn't break through. What I have to do is back off and let events unfold as they are going to. I went back and talked with a case manager to see if other agencies would come through with money to pay this woman's rent so we could give her another month to try to get things together. But other professionals don't know how to deal with these clients. I had to do a mini education on how to interact with her and how to intervene with her. A real important part of my job is to educate coworkers and colleagues that don't know anything and are really scared by addiction. I try to give them the tools that they need to be successful in their interventions. I also went to the Seattle housing authority, which had made the original referral, and lobbied for them to give this woman another chance. I didn't really think she'd follow through on it, but I'd gotten her to agree to a protective payee the following month. I asked them if they would agree to not evict her if we managed to come up with the first month's rent and if she would agree to get a payee the following month. They agreed not to evict her. I was buying time to give her the opportunity to get back into treatment. That's a pretty typical case.

I run three groups in the housing project. I have a grandmothers' group that I call the Wise Women's Circle, the gathering of grandmothers. They are grandmothers who are raising grandchildren because their adult children are involved with alcohol and drugs. Although sometimes, it's grandmothers who are in recovery and are alienated from their adult children because they've been involved with alcohol and drugs. I also have a codependency group for women. I find this really useful for women who are single moms, women who are in abusive relationships, and women who are in recovery. It's about setting limits. And I have a "coping with change" group, which is for men and women who have at least a few days of not drinking or using. This group runs the range from people with 3 months of being clean and sober to a woman who has 13 years of recovery. It includes everything in between. All three groups are small.

It is extremely challenging to keep encouraging people to come to these groups. When I'm feeling discouraged, I think I'm just like the little boy with a finger in the dike, and everything is getting ready to spill out. I think I'm wasting my time here, I'm not doing any good. Invariably, when I get to that place, something will happen. The last time that I got there, I came out from doing a group and only two women had shown up for the group. I was leaving and saw this woman walking toward me. She says, "Pat, you do that group for women, right?" I said yeah. She said, "I've been wanting to come to your group for about 6 months." It turns out that I had done a group training for women who were trying to gain the skills they need to get up off their butts and go back to work. Apparently, she had been in that group. I didn't remember her, but she remembered me. Apparently, she'd been watching me and listening to reports about the groups I was doing. So my reputation gets around.

Let me tell you what keeps me going. I work in an arena where there's a lot of toxicity and chaos. There's an enormous amount of violence. Every week, somebody gets murdered. This has a terrific impact on everybody around here when that happens. The rest of my life is so wonderfully stable and solid and nurturing. You can't give out what you don't have. I need—from a self-care perspective—for all the rest of my life to be filling up that well. Then, I can go in there every day and pull out the best I have to give to the individual and the community. When I go home at the end of the day, I'm very grateful for my life. When I left that little boy whose mother was a heroin addict, later that day, I picked up my grandson because I was taking care of him for 4 nights a week. I got out of the car, I walked in the door, and there he was on the other side of the door, saying "Hi, Hi," happy to see me. I just got so full.

Today, I look more at the political world in terms of what's my responsibility. I'm at a place where I take responsibility for my life. I take responsibility for being politically active or being socially aware and the whole bit. I've learned that I can't do anything about the whole system. I can do something about me. I can take responsibility for all the different aspects of my life and my part in it. I can feel good about what I am trying to do to the best of my abilities, one day at a time. In terms of my work, I just do the best that I can and to try to inspire people to have a sense of hope about their lives in the midst of all their chaos.

❖ KATHY LORTIE

Thirteen years ago, I had a baby with Down's syndrome. When she was 2½ months old, she got sick and had to go the hospital. She had bacterial pneumonia. I took her home and gave her oral antibiotics, but the bacteria started growing again. Two days later, the baby got meningitis. We had to rush her back to the hospital. They flew us from the community hospital in our hometown to Children's Hospital in Washington, DC.

I still remember when we went into the emergency room. The first thing a nurse asked us when we walked in was if we wanted a social worker. I knew at that moment the baby was going to die. They don't ask you in the ER if you want a social worker unless it is really, really bad. So I said, "No." I thought, "To hell with this. If I have a social worker, then the baby will die. So, no, I don't want a social worker." The staff called a social worker anyway. This woman came in and took us to a special room. That is a bad sign, too. I used to work in an ER, and when they put you in a special room, you know it is bad. When they call the social worker in, it is even worse. We met with the social worker. She came in, it was a Saturday night, and sat down beside me. She did not say a word. She didn't even tell us who she was. She was obviously upset that our baby was dying. The whole time, I felt I was there to protect her from my emotions because she was having a hard time dealing with my baby dying. I felt like I had to be the strong one for her.

After a while, they took us up to the intensive care unit and put us in another special room with the social worker again. I really wanted this woman to leave us alone so that I could talk to my husband and we could deal with what was going on. She just sat there the whole time. For hours, just sat there. She didn't have a clue as to what to say or what to do for us. When the baby died, we were not given the opportunity to say that enough was enough. They just kept trying to save this dying baby until it got to the point where the baby was so sick that she bled out. All of her blood vessels broke, and she bled from every part of her body, her ears and her nose, her pores. It was a horrible death. While that happened, I never got to see my baby in the intensive care unit. Then afterwards, they made me go in and look. It was the most horrible thing that I'd ever seen because it was my child. It didn't even look like a child anymore. I got very upset, and I screamed at the staff. They took me back to see the social worker. All she could say was that the police might want to investigate this because my baby came in and died within 24 hours of admission. The social worker didn't give me any information, had nothing encouraging to say whatsoever, just left it at that. I had to leave the hospital with no child.

At that point, I thought, "I can do better than this." So while staying home with my young children, I looked for things to do where I could work with mothers and babies. I became a childbirth instructor and started working with families, with the long-term goal of eventually going back, after my children were older, to become a social worker in a hospital. I currently have the job of working in a pediatric unit in a hospital. When moms come in and their children or babies die, I know what it is like. I know when they want to be left alone, and I leave them alone. I know when they need help and support. I've developed a packet of information that I give them about what grieving is like, what they can expect to feel like, a list of funeral homes, and information on how to plan their baby's funeral. I give them reading materials and a list of support groups that they can contact and ideas for memorials. I ask them if they want me to make hand prints or foot prints to remember their child. I have quilts that some people have made for us that I give to the family so they can wrap their baby in it, or they can keep the quilt for a memory. I have a Polaroid camera, and I offer to take pictures of them and their baby. The staff also always tries to give the parents the option of holding the baby, before the baby bleeds out or something like that. I try to talk to the mom and encourage her to be able to do that. I know it is hard, but it is a really beautiful gift that parents can give themselves and their child. That is usually how the babies die at this hospital, in their mothers' arms.

In my job, I also know what it feels like to have a handicapped child, a sick child, and to be that stressed and to be doing it alone. We had no family. Even though my baby only lived 3 months, I remember those 3 months as being so intense and stressful. In the hospital, I know that some people have the idea a social worker's job is to empower people to take care of themselves. When you have a sick child and you are that stressed out, you can't be empowered; you need somebody to do it for you. I'm there, and I'm the one with the energy. I'm the one who doesn't have any problems. I can do things for people to get them back to the point where they can start doing things for themselves—instead of me just going in and handing somebody a phone number and saying,

"Here is a resource for you in the community; you follow up on it." I'm going to make sure that they get that resource. I put a lot of effort into finding out what they need and making sure that they have a way to get what they need. I will have the other workers come into the hospital to see the mom. I don't tell the mom that she is going to take a sick baby and get on a bus and go down to the Department of Economic Security (welfare) office. I call up and say, "You need to come to see this person here at the hospital because they can't get down there."

There is one case I remember that sort of illustrates all of this. A doctor asked me to see a family that he described as a social disaster. The patient was a 7-month-old baby boy who needed a liver transplant. The parents were poor and had three other children. They did not have much social support. The father worked more than full-time at various jobs to support the family. The mother did the baby's care and handled all of the other family responsibilities. But she was having a hard time doing it all, and the baby wasn't growing well. When I tried to talk to them about their problems, they said, "We don't need to talk about our problems. We need help doing something about them." The mother needed someone to help her with the baby and cooking and laundry. I worked for weeks with this family. I had community workers come to the hospital to help the family get services. I walked this mother through the process of applying for state-funded in-home care. I fought the insurance company for appropriate home health nursing. I got them into better low-income housing.

For a while, things went well. They were able to care for the baby at home, and he grew. Then he got an infection and had to be admitted. He ended up in intensive care. It was really sad. Everyone knew he was dying, but his mother had a very hard time letting go. The baby was on total life support, on a breathing machine and on medicines to keep his heart beating. There was no hope. We talked to the parents about how they wanted their child to die, and they decided to withdraw the life support. I remember, the mother looked at me and asked, "Am I going to be alright?" And I remembered how I had survived my own baby dying, and I said, "Yes, you are going to be OK." This baby died in his parents' arms while they sang to him. After he died, his mother wanted to bathe and dress him. I was in the room with the nurse then, and the nurse took the baby from his mother to put him back on the bed. But the baby was still connected to tubes and wires, and it was hard for the nurse to handle alone. She looked at me and said, "I need help; take him." I reached out and took this dead baby from the nurse and put him on the bed. Then we washed him and dressed him and took pictures. Some people think this sounds awful, but there are times when I can do things for people—put together a discharge, find resources and information for families, offer this kind of help and emotional support—that really makes a difference in their lives.

Most of my clients have incredibly difficult lives, but I really love working with them, with poor children and their families, helping their families care for them, to get what they need to keep their kids healthy, to help when the kids are really sick. There is so much hope there for the future. But it is getting harder. I look at the lives of some of the families I work with: The parents have little support, few resources, and sick children. They are often doing their best, and if they work, they can't get health insurance for their kids because they make too much money to qualify for state-funded Medicaid— $5 an hour, that's too much. Now, there is welfare reform, and the mothers have to work. We recently had one chronically ill baby whose mother had to go off welfare and get a job. The baby got admitted to the hospital with an overdose of her medicine. She had three different caregivers so mom could work odd hours, and each did not realize the others had already given the baby the medicine, so the baby got three doses. The doctor said, "Where is the mother?" I said, "She's working. Remember, now we have welfare reform, so she can't leave her job and come to the hospital to discuss this problem with us, or she will be fired and the baby won't get to eat because they can't get food stamps anymore." You know, I don't see welfare queens working the system. I see a lot of really poor people trying to feed their children and keep them healthy. It is stressful for them, and this stress can contribute to child abuse. I see a lot of child abuse, too.

I had a string of memorable cases last winter when there was a bunch of child protective services cases involving babies. We had a baby who had come in that had obviously been strangled. We figured out what must have happened: Someone had grabbed the front of her baby clothes and pulled and twisted them in a way that cut off the circulation to her head. That is the only thing that would explain the injuries that she had to her brain. I don't think her parents were bad people, though—just young and poor and very stressed. After that, we had a baby come in whose mom was in a methadone program. She was not doing real well in the program because she was also taking heroin and breast feeding the baby. The baby drank heroin in the breast milk and died from it. Then, in the same week, a family brought their baby in with a serious head injury. Some cultures think that if the soft spot on the baby's head looks like it is going down, they need to make it go back out again, so some people will take their thumb and press on the top of the roof of the baby's mouth. Some people will take the baby to a faith healer who holds the baby by the ankles and shakes the baby upside down to make the soft spot come back out again. The baby suffered some pretty serious brain damage from being shaken while being held upside down.

Sometimes, I ask myself why am I doing this? Wouldn't I rather have a different kind of job where I didn't have to get so emotionally involved and wouldn't work so hard, and I could make more money? But you know, the one time in my life when I needed a lot of help, I had friends who gave that to me. Now that I am no longer in that position, it's my turn to be able to give that to someone else. It helps me to be able to deal with what happened to me to be able to turn around and say, "OK, I survived it, and I'm OK." And because I'm OK, I can take all that happened to me and find some meaning in it. That is important because when one of your children dies, one of the things you do is to sit around and wonder if there is a God. Why did this happen and how can God do this to little children? But this is just what happens to people in their life—all people, not just me—and we are here to help each other, to provide support and caring for other people. How can we not care for each other? How can we not provide health insurance for all children? How can we not ensure that all children get enough to eat? Life is tough, bad things happen to all of us. We need to be there and be strong for each other.

❖ ROBERT (BOB) KAFES

I was born in Philadelphia in 1942. I never knew that social work existed until I came to New York in 1965 after spending most of my life in theater. I had worked in the theater from the time I was 11 years old and through my undergraduate work at Boston University where I earned my bachelor's in fine arts in 1965. During that time, in order to escape from what we now call an extremely dysfunctional family, and in order to cope with my homosexuality and come out and deal with all of that, I found wonderful people in the theater who, because I was so young, took very good care of me. They were kind and extremely nurturing in a way my parents couldn't be.

In 1965, during Johnson's Great Society, there was an advertisement in the New York Times for caseworkers for the city of New York. The Department of Welfare had just changed it's name to the Department of Social Services, and they were going with a much broader approach—not simply giving people money, but really trying to understand social problems that precipitated clients going on welfare. I passed the civil service exam and started my first social work job.

I worked for the Department of Social Services for 9 months, and I just loved it. I had a wonderful teacher named Phyllis Simmons. I remember her because she inspired about social work. I really felt called. I'll never forget one of my clients who had 10 children. She had a fire in her apartment, and I helped her. I got her and her kids a place to live. I enjoyed talking with the old people who were on my caseloads. I enjoyed helping people with real-life issues and needs, like planning for school, finding housing, and finding food. It was real life.

But I left the Department of Social Services one summer because I was scheduled to direct a production of *Gentlemen Prefer Blondes*. At the end of the summer, I didn't have a job, and I struggled along. Miracle of all miracles, I was hired by the New York Light House for the Blind, and I worked there for 4 years. I left this work for two more stints to direct summer plays. When I would go away for the summer and get these great reviews for the shows that I directed, I actually felt sad and depressed. I just didn't feel the glow of triumph that I had previously.

At the same time, my mother, who had been mentally ill and diagnosed with paranoid schizophrenia, was hospitalized in a state hospital. Also, my lover at the time left me. I was abandoned and alone in New York. I didn't know what to do, but I had a very good friend who I owe my life to. I was extremely depressed, and he helped me get into therapy. One Thanksgiving weekend, he practically carried me to a therapist's office. I was seen at a low-cost, sliding-scale clinic in New York City called Community Guidance Service. This was when clinical social work became real to me personally—it saved my life. Had there been no sliding scale for me when I needed services, I would have been dead. I would not have survived. In any case, through my therapy, I began to sort out that the theater had been a wonderful refuge for me when I was growing up and terrific place to be then. But it wasn't what I needed as a young adult. What I was coming to terms with was that I loved social work. I loved the realness of it. I loved the people that I was aiding, and I loved the profession.

Eventually, my goal was to enter Yeshiva University School of Social Work, for my master's degree. In my 5 years of social work, I had worked with the vast mosaic that is New York City—the wonderful people, colors, and ethnic groups, the whole dimensions of peoples that are a part of New York City. But I wanted to learn about Jewish social work, Jewish community service. Part of the school's requirement was four semesters in Jewish social values and Jewish social philosophy. Even though I was educated Jewishly, and bar mitzvahed and confirmed, basically I knew nothing about my own people because I had never wanted to be in religious school. I learned nothing in all those past years, going to religious school. I was now 27 years old, and I felt I had wasted my entire life in the theater. I felt that I'd better get on the stick here and really get back to school and study hard and get a career and get my act together. So I went to Yeshiva, and I loved it.

I eventually went into private practice in New York City for 16 years. I feel it takes at least 10 years to get your feet on the ground as a therapist. It took me 10 years after my institute training to feel competent. They don't call it a practice for nothing. We are always practicing. I used to joke, "Don't we ever get it right? When does it become perfect?" I really do believe that practice simply makes more practice. I've been in the field for 33 years, and I think this is what keeps me alive in the field—the understanding that our work is always practicing. We are always learning and growing. We are always engaging in new dimensions of experience, new learning. I think it is the most exciting field in the world.

I think that, over the years, what I've learned is how to be with people, to really trust the therapeutic process, to allow a person to be, and to trust my being with them in a real way—not to feel like I have to do something, or change something, or make a difference, or be something that I'm not. As I said, it took a lot of painful growing on my part. There were many times when I would feel that I could do nothing. Or I would worry that this person is going to commit suicide, or this person is going to go off the deep end in one way or another, or I ought to be doing more. For me, to trust what I'm doing—to trust that I have begun to ask the right questions to deepen my relationship with a client, to trust that we are engaged together in a process, and that process involves helping another person understand himself—that feels like enough to me. I have to understand my own limitations, my own need for values. I have to understand myself, who I am as a person. One of the things I told my students was that if you are a clinical social worker, you have to have integrity. Be yourself with integrity; be authentic.

I was in private practice during the AIDS epidemic in 1983, and most of my practice was with gay men. Maybe that is one of the reasons that I was so successful, because homosexuality was considered a disease at that time, so there were few therapists to go to who weren't trying to change people's sexual orientation.

Maybe one of my claims to fame is that I was one of the first "out" therapists in New York City back in 1972. I was a gay therapist. In any case, my reputation grew because clients were referred to me from an agency called Homosexual Community Counseling Center. I also had regular-fee patients, but most of my practice was gay men. And then, people started getting sick. They started having colds that wouldn't go away. There was an article in a New York magazine about an epidemic, a strange disease going around called, "gay-related immune deficiency." Then, there was a New York Times article, and it became a very frightening time. It was horrible because here were strapping, healthy young men who would come in with marks on their faces or losing weight, experiencing night sweats, having diarrhea. It was a horror show that nobody knew how to view. None of us had learned anything about this in school. Human service professionals from all stripes would call each other and ask, "What are you doing? What is this?" We would all try to work together to understand this thing. I might be with a client, and he might mention a name of somebody I knew casually—an acquaintance from a bar, from a dance, from a political function, or whatever—who died. I would sit in my office week after week and hear about people who had died.

There was a phrase that another social worker, Mike Schernoff, termed *bereavement overload*. This is when you get overloaded with bereavement because you are facing it so much. You go to memorial services over and over again. You hear over and over again about people you know who have died. It's a horrible grieving. The grieving never stops because you can't complete grief for one because there are more to come, so there is no end to the grief. There were many people who accused me and who were angry with me for leaving New York City at that time because they really felt that I was abandoning them in the face of AIDS. Maybe that is true. It wasn't my conscious reason for leaving New York, but maybe I just couldn't take it anymore. It was a lot to take.

Incidentally, social work was in the forefront of the AIDS epidemic. But for me, the reason I feel so at home in the profession is because it is so very *me*. I was always the kind of kid who was very interested in helping people, listening to people. I was the kid who the other kids would tell their troubles to. I look back at my life and see the roots are there. I was always interested in the vulnerable and helping those who were more vulnerable than I was. I just wanted to be there for them.

I wish people knew how great social work is. Social work has a very poor public image. I don't think people know what it is. We don't see social workers on TV on the talk shows, on the Sunday morning political shows, or in the news or commentaries. We do so much. I was redoing my resume recently, and I thought, "What if I hadn't touched these people? What if we had never met? What if social work didn't exist as a profession?" I can't imagine what kind of country or world this would be. I think we are too modest. I don't think we give ourselves credit or create the kind of public image that other professions create for themselves, like doctors and lawyers. We don't boast enough! What we do hear about is the negative aspect of the profession. We are too self-effacing. You know what I would love to have happen? I would love to have a child say, "I want to be a social worker when I grow up."

❖ LEVONNE GADDY

Everything that I've done in social work, every type of work that I've done, has been a part of my own journey, my way of dealing with my own demons, my own past, my own trauma. I'm 43 years old today, and I'm probably going to be working for at least another 20 years or so. I couldn't imagine that I would want to have anything to do with a profession if it didn't enhance my own personal growth, personal from the inside out. Social work does that.

I was born in a small, rural community in the South. I was raised as an African American, a black person. Of course, you can tell from the way that I look that I'm not all African American, but in the South, there is that one-drop rule, where if you have a drop of black blood, then you are a black person. My parents were both biracial, and they identified as black people. So I grew up in an African American culture, and I am very thankful to have had that strong identity and that life. I wouldn't do anything differently, even though that experience caused a lot of conflict in my life because I didn't look like other black people. It was also in the '60s when there was a lot of the black power stuff going on and a lot of racial conflict. Everywhere that I went, conflict was the name of the game.

I decided that I was going to go for my dream, which was to live in sunny Southern California and go to beach parties just like I'd seen on TV. I left North Carolina, and I went to Los Angeles. At one point, the way I think got me in trouble. I got fired from a secretarial job. I didn't understand it at that time because I was young and naive. I went into a traditional corporation as a secretary, and I refused to carry coffee and do the normal secretarial things. I just said, "Well, you know, I've got a lot of work to do. I don't even drink coffee, and I don't take breaks, so you guys get your own coffee." You know? It just seemed normal and natural to me to do that. The next thing I knew, I was fired. One of the people there had told me beforehand that I'd better watch out, and I didn't know what he was talking about. He told me that I was the kind of person who needed to be out of the corporate world and be in a social work type of world. Nothing made sense to me at that point about what this person was saying. I was just blown away by this whole experience. That was my first encounter with the words "social worker."

I started working at a free clinic as a sexual reproduction counselor, which was a good thing for me to learn about. I also volunteered at a suicide prevention center. These things were issues in my life, so I started educating myself and helping others. I decided that I would like to make some money at this, so I went back to school. I don't feel that I consciously chose a lot of my path at the beginning. I went to grad school and had some good experiences and field placements. Then, I was out in the world. My first job was in child protection, and I was seeing abused children . . . children abused in every way possible. It broke my heart to see those kids.

Next, I moved into adoption, where I was trying to find permanent homes for kids. That was a mixed bag because for some kids, great things happened, and they ended up with great families. But for other kids, my decisions about who they should be with didn't always work out. There was this 10-year-old girl who loved her foster family and her foster family loved her. But I insisted that she needed to be adopted. I was into making adoptions happen. I found a family that seemed right for her, a man and a woman. She would be their only child. They shared the same racial, ethnic sort of makeup. She resisted, but then she did end up with this family. I left that job, and my friend who was there took over my caseload. She told me many months later, "Remember this girl? Her adopted father was sexually molesting her, and the mother was living out of the home but would come back for the follow-up visits and pretend that she still lived there." Here was this girl living alone with this man who was treating her like his prostitute. My heart hurts today for that decision and what happened to that girl. The good thing is that the foster family still wanted her, and she still wanted to be with them, so she was able to go back to them. I think that is my most sad social work experience.

At the same time, there was a boy that I just fell in love with. He was 5 years old and the most wonderful kid that I could ever imagine on this earth. I just loved this kid. One day, he told me that his foster family was beating him. Now, I can't take him home with me. All I can do is try to get him out of there as fast as possible. So I did. I got him out of there pretty quickly without letting them know that I was aware of the beatings so they wouldn't take it out on him more. He ended up with a family that I think is a good family. They have provided a stable home for him. To me, that is one of my better stories.

There is always that balance, especially in working with kids, about how close I'm willing to be and what kind of boundaries I need to keep, how disengaged I should be and how engaged I'll allow myself to be. For me, this has been one of the hardest things in my work. I want to care for the children; I want them to like me, and I want to like them. I want to have connections; I want to know what happens to their lives. It was not a great thing for me to get so invested in that little boy's life because I think he saw me as his "psychological mother." And since I didn't adopt him or have him live with me, it was like another mother abandoned him. I didn't keep him for myself, and

I didn't take him into my life. That is something that I need to make amends for to this young man. He's 17 now, and I need to apologize for that.

In 1983, I started the first multiracial support organization that Los Angeles had. The second largest city in this country, a metro area with every kind of culture, ethnicity, racial person you could ever imagine, and they have nothing for multiracial people. I was dissatisfied with having to always choose: I'll go to this black thing, and I'll go to that dominant culture thing, always having to choose between the different pieces of myself. I thought I had had enough of that, and I wanted my own thing. I wanted multiracial because that is what I am. What I started has grown into a viable organization today.

I'm preparing to go into working again with children. What is different for me now is that I'm very aware that I'm not going to be able to do this work by myself. I'm going to use my coworkers to help me see what is a reasonable balance of involvement and disengagement. I'm going to use the people I'm with, other professionals, to help guide me. In the past, that is not something that I've allowed. I've been pretty independent and self-directed. But there is a place for allowing others because sometimes they can see these issues more clearly than I can.

A lot of things in my life I haven't chosen. I came here without a job, and my husband and I chose a part of the city out here in the country. We had no idea what work was available. But we discovered a treatment center a few minutes away that specializes in addictions. I have never wanted to work with addictions, even though addiction issues pop up in every social work job. But I still was not willing to do that work exclusively. So there I was. I sent out 25 applications to different places, and nobody was interested in me. Then I go over to the addictions center, and they hire me within the hour. I knew that I could do almost anything, but I didn't want to do anything related to alcoholism. But here I am again! Not really looking for these things, but there it is. It's exactly the work that I needed to be doing; it's exactly the work that I needed to be doing with myself. I had all this baggage from my own life in the addictions model that I hadn't really understood because I hadn't had that experience.

I'm in a 12-step recovery program now, and I'm starting to realize that the higher power in my life has always directed my course, even though I've tried so hard to be in control. I'm really just starting more and more to trust this process of just being in the world and being who I am and letting things happen.

We don't have to be perfect human beings to aid someone else along their path. Somebody said to me, "You don't have to have all your shit worked out, but you do have to know where your shit is."

8

Keeping the Vision Alive

❖ JANE JACOBS WALTON

I always had an interest in working in corrections. It's kind of closed in and a little confined for me, but other than that, it's interesting. I almost never get tired of reading about inmates' offenses and the portion of their pre-sentence report that talks about their personal history and how they were raised. Most of their backgrounds are obvious. They came from broken homes where their fathers beat them. They come from lives and families that are dysfunctional. But there are some whose upbringing appeared to be stable and normal, and you wonder if they got hooked up with a bad group or what happened? I always start thinking about what could lead them into a life of crime.

I am a case manager. I think my official title is Correctional Treatment Specialist. I do discharge planning, and that kind of thing, as people are getting ready to go back into the community. My job is very technical, not really what you might think of as a classic social worker, although there is social work built into what I do. It comes through daily contact with the inmates, preparing them for release and such. I don't do therapy with the inmates. We have a separate department for that, and therapeutic sessions are available. I make a difference in a different way, by being able to provide them with daily resources and maybe small comforts that they wouldn't otherwise have if I weren't there.

I originally wanted to do community corrections, which is parole-probation work with offenders in the community. I still would like to do that work someday, instead of working behind the fences. Behind the fences, you go to work and carry keys, and you go through the institution doors that close behind you. Then you are inside, behind these double fences all day. I guess anyone who works in any office is inside for the whole day. But there is something about work in the prison that makes you feel like you are an inmate for the day. It just seems more confining. Everything is obviously locked. My office is in a housing unit where the inmates live. While I'm in my office, I keep the door open so the inmates know that I'm there. They are free to come in as long as I'm not busy on the phone or something. Then, if I leave, I have to close my door and lock it. If I want to use the restroom, I lock my door, unlock another door, and I lock it back. It's a different way to spend 8 hours a day.

I can think of both good and bad experiences. In terms of a bad one, I was once preparing an inmate for release, for parole, and he didn't have a place to go. He talked about how he had heard that probation officers could arrange for people to get hotel vouchers, places for them to stay. So I thought, "OK. You can get a hotel voucher, and you'll be fine." But I said to him, "You still need to give me a release address so they'll approve your parole." He gave me an address, and I sent it to the parole commission and he got paroled. I later found out that after release, that inmate committed suicide. The address he had given me was a bogus address, the former address of a dead relative of his. It made me think more about getting inmates ready for release. It isn't necessarily my job to investigate the information they give me; that is something that the probation officer would do. But it caused me to pay more attention to their community connections and what they have going for them on the outside instead of thinking, "His release date is January 10, and that's all that I have to do with him." A person lost his life when maybe that would not have happened if I had been a little more—I don't know—accommodating, or if I had foreseen what was going to happen. Maybe there was something I could have done to prevent it. But this was early in my career and I had a lot of learning to do, and I made that mistake.

It's important to realize that you do have important responsibilities. In my job, people come for just everything you can imagine, because they are so isolated from their families. The only phone calls they can make are collect, and lots of them have long-distance blocks. I had an inmate who wanted to call his wife to wish her a happy birthday, and she wasn't home to receive the collect call. He wanted that message left so that when she got home from celebrating her birthday, it would be there from him. I said, "OK, I'll give you a 30-second phone call." My boss was there at the time, and he just laughed at me. He still teases me about this inmate. He was a relatively obnoxious inmate, but it didn't matter to me. I just thought, "This is part of his life, part of his rehabilitation, to have that relationship when he gets out of prison." I know from being a wife and being a human being, a call on your birthday like that is really important, and I knew that he was having some trouble with his marriage, as many of the inmates do. Giving him the call was a small thing I could do.

Because I'm a woman, one of the bigger issues I've faced in my job is being guarded about the relationships that I have with the inmates on my caseload—or the inmates in general, being careful that my interaction with them is always professional, that I don't feel that I've crossed the line and nobody else would feel that I've crossed the line. I've been here 7 years, and I think I'm still learning how to be friendly with the inmates without feeling like I was leading them on. I have to keep that wall up: "I think that you're a nice person and pleasant, but I'm your case manager, and I'm also a correctional worker." That's hard. We have to be disciplinarians when we receive incident reports. We have to call inmates in, have a hearing, decide if they are guilty or not guilty, apply appropriate sanctions, and then send them on their way and hope that the next day, they are happy with us. That is hard. It's not natural. It's not human nature to be an authority figure and then a friend. Although, in a way, you are sort of the disciplinarian and then you are the one who hugs and tucks him in.

I have never felt like I was in danger here. The staff members are great. The institution is equipped in plenty of ways that make you feel safe. Also, I don't think I have a particularly antagonistic relationship with the inmate population. I think that, in general, they are comfortable with me as much as I am with them. There is no way to ensure that you are not going to have an inmate who loses it. So even though I feel that I have a good relationship with them, you could always have the one inmate who flips out and comes after you. That has never happened to me, and hopefully it never will. But if it did, there is plenty of recourse. I would never put myself in a situation where I would be in danger.

My work has probably negatively influenced my view of humankind. I'm exposed to the people who have had really unfortunate experiences, at least in their recent years and possibly during their formative years. It tends to make you untrusting, for one thing. Every time I go to the bank, all I can think about is who is there to rob the bank.

At our prison, the American Friends Service Committee brings in a program called Alternatives to Violence. It's a national program, offered to inmates on weekends, and I recommend that my inmates take the program. Often, when we have team reviews, they will tell me, "I don't need to go to the Alternatives to Violence Program because I'm not a violent person." I tell them the program is not named appropriately, in my opinion, because it teaches a lot of living skills. There's a lot about conflict resolution and about different ways of feeling in various life situations: how to live in harmony more effectively with your family, with your friends, how to conduct yourself on a job and not become angry and quit when your boss tells you that you didn't sweep the floor right. It teaches them different ways of addressing their problems, different ways of thinking about their actions. That program is the only one we have that gives them a different way of thinking about themselves.

There aren't many happy stories in the work that I do. It's always happy when you have any kind of success or make any changes in an inmate's life. Like giving the call for the inmate's wife's birthday or working hard to get a placement in a half-way house that is successful, and an inmate gets the placement that he wants. Those things mean a lot to them. They don't seem like much to us when you have 140 inmates, and he's one, and you are working on 20 halfway house placements. You just think, "OK, that's done," and then you move on. But if you look back at them and really pay attention to the work that you are doing, there are a lot of things that I don't feel happiness about, but they do.

I really like my job. I like the people I work for and the people I work with. I like the organization. There is also the issue of working for the federal government, which has its advantage with regard to benefits and retirement. Even without that, I really enjoy my work right now. It hasn't always been that way. I went through a couple of years where I didn't have interest in it, and I didn't like what I was doing. I think part of it was getting experience and learning about how to develop rapport with the inmates. And finding my identity was a part of it.

It was a struggle, though. Hearing a lot of negative feedback was a big part of it: hearing it from inmates, hearing it from other workers, hearing it from my boss saying, "They think you are unresponsive." I didn't realize that I was giving that impression. I was working so hard at trying to stay professional and trying to be a strong correctional worker that I didn't give myself a chance to be human. Everyone picked up on that really well. There are people who say that you can be bold, that you can be a hard-ass correction worker and then also be their friend. I don't believe it, personally. There are people who say that you need both types of workers. You need to have the hard-ass type, and you need to have the more human type (which is hopefully what I've become). But I don't believe that, either. Everybody can be human in what they do. It's hard, and there are a lot of people who work here—guards and others—who haven't found a way to be human in how they deal with the inmates. It's tough sometimes.

❖ CAROLYN JACKSON

Being a social worker means that I use my skills for problem resolution: How do I figure out the best thing that I can do on behalf of my client?

I would like to share with you a story about a client who had a history of substance abuse. This was someone who had a history of sexual abuse with her own son, who had a history of being a prostitute, but who totally turned her life around. I'm not saying that my intervention was all that caused this gorgeous, attractive, intelligent woman to turn her life around, but I know that I had a hand in it. To know and realize that people change over time is gratifying, particularly given their problems.

You would think, "How can this person do it? What motivation does she have?" She came from a family background that was disorganized and pathological. Fortunately, she was able to get away from that background and was removed from that context when I worked with her. She got involved with some government-sponsored programs for employment, school, and residential treatment. Those things were available, and she took advantage of them. After she got out of the residential treatment center, she stopped drinking, stopped using drugs, and because of the job assistance, she was slowly able to move up. She went to the local junior college and improved her English, typing, and other skills.

She got stronger after her therapy. She went into therapy on her own to deal with some basic life issues and problems that had plagued her for a long time. She was able to take advantage of the resources that were available. Why she decided to do this, I couldn't tell you; she is the only one who can answer that. But I have seen this woman over the years since I've worked with her, in different social environments, and she has shared on more than one occasion, "I still hear you talking to me."

That is gratifying to me, and the system worked for someone in this case. But the person also worked, and that is the key thing. I try to empower people to know that they have strengths and can utilize them. She had worked with another therapist before she came to see me who kept telling her that she had to get rid of the skills that she used as a prostitute. I said, "That's impossible." Those same skills can be utilized in a different way in terms of sizing up situations, whether they are employment or social situations. Not that she is looking for "John," but she is looking at body language, looking at speech patterns, looking at the actual words that people use to get things done. She did that as a prostitute. There was no reason she should ignore skills that she had developed. She was able to use those skills to her advantage. Certainly, they could be useful in dealing with employers, her coworkers, and those kinds of things. They were resources for her in a work environment where she was earning a legitimate income and moving up in the occupational structure, and she certainly did move up.

I still remember from my years in school how important it is to start where the client is. I had to start where she was. Because she was socially deficient in a number of areas, I did a lot of—some people might say trite or mundane—exercises. She couldn't balance a checkbook, so she would have financial problems. In that case, you teach her how to balance a checkbook. With regard to job hunting, she would look under "clerk." She wouldn't look at the heading of the job listing in the paper.

She would just look for anything that looked like a clerk-type position. She didn't know how to prepare for an interview for a formal job; I used to make her role-play: "OK, go outside the door and come back in. I'll interview you."

She has told me I don't know how many times since then, "You know, I hated you for making me do that?" I said, "Yeah. But you did it, didn't you?" All I wanted to show her was that there were options and that she could develop the skills to exercise those options. The better she got at doing that, the happier she became. It was like she began to have faith that it was possible to change something in her life.

I used to talk to her about her attire. She was an African American woman who had needle marks on her arms and legs, and they embarrassed her. She always wore pants. I said, "You cannot continue to always wear pants if you are going to get the professional job that you want." This was a gorgeous, beautifully figured woman, but she still had to wear skirts. You know what I'm saying? Being African American myself, I am familiar with certain health care products that we use to minimize stretch marks from pregnancy and from dark skin patches on the skin. I said, "Try some of these things," and she did. One day, she came to the office for her appointment after wearing pants forever. I opened my door, and I could see the reception area. She walked up to the reception desk, and the receptionist said, "Your client is here." I opened the door, and she was standing there in a skirt. What a happy day for her!

Things that are related to her self-image were so basic and practical to this woman's self-esteem. If I hadn't been able to talk about certain things, she wouldn't have thought that those were important, yet those were the things that were keeping her back because she thought that she couldn't rise above them. I was assertive and said, "Are you aware of this and are you aware of that?" When you work with someone for a while, they begin to have confidence in you, confidence that the things that you are saying to them are not put-downs. People are very sensitive. They are also vulnerable. After working with her for a while, she could see that I was not out to put her down and that there was some validity in the things that I was sharing with her. Some of those things just seem basic and practical, but I think when you function from a position of "do no harm" and try to be helpful, you go where you need to go. That is where the client is. Sometimes, the client is not able to admit that they are there, but you can go there.

When we first role-played "I'm an employer and you are coming for a job," we didn't start with what kind of job; we started with how you enter. I told her, "You are sauntering in the door. You aren't looking at the person. You aren't offering to shake hands. You are sitting in a slouched position. Already, you've given that employer a negative impression of yourself. Let's do it again." So out the door she would go. The day I talked to her about the bank and about her finances, I said, "You know, bank people are supposed to be able to help you with some of this." The primary thing I taught her was that there are resources she could use to get things done in her life.

Whenever I work with clients like this, my whole style is about empowerment. I have to ask the clients about themselves: "You look like a shy person to me. Is that true?" The body language, the voice, will go with that. Then, you can pursue that, ask why, ask whether this is effective or ineffective for them. Therapy is faster when it is done that way. We have to lay something out for clients in terms of how they can succeed, without being pejorative or negative. We know that if they continue to go down this particular road, they are not likely to succeed. So you work from the strengths that the person has. You talk to that, when you share with someone: "You know, look at your behavior here." With the HMOs and case management and cutbacks on funds, the client has got to make some progress. This is not Freudian psychoanalysis that goes on for years. Most of the clients we work with cannot even begin to afford that. Yet that is what they think therapy is, and that is what they try to avoid. I'm going to come at the client fairly directly, because people come to me of their own volition. They are not uncooperative clients. If you come to me of your own volition, usually it's because somebody else saw me first and referred you. I say, "If Mary referred you, Mary told you how I work, right?" "Yes." "What did Mary tell you?" "Well, that you are direct. You use role-play. You really want to see things change." "Right. You did your homework." "Right." "Understand that up front, because I'm not changing that style." People who go into therapy want to feel better for the most part. I let them know,

> I don't live those other hours of the week that you are not in my office. I only live that one hour with you. You've got to do something out there on your own so you may as well try something different, the exercises or whatever I may give you to do. You also have the right to say to me, "You are moving too fast, and I didn't get it. I know you talked about that last

week, but somehow I lost it." Fine. Then I'll go back; but don't tell me that 5 weeks in a row, because then I need to figure out whether there is something else going on.

Everybody needs to be affirmed, not just our clients. That is what is wonderful to me. The key is how a person gets a handle on their stuff. I'm empowering, helping people take control of their lives.

❖ KATHRYN GRAYBILL

When I was a child, one of my role models was my father, who was a country doctor in the rural Midwest. He did home visits, and I would often ride around with him to see his patients. I think a lot of my values came from that. He also was what they called the "Insanity Commissioner" for that small county, so I heard a lot about the people in the community who had mental health problems and were termed "crazy." That led me to be interested in pursuing work in mental health, and eventually I got my MSW.

I don't do direct service anymore. I'm a clinical director, and a lot of what I do is to coordinate staffing of different agencies that are mandated to provide services for children. A lot of the cases with children involve maltreatment or abuse from different members of the family. The child becomes involved with different agencies, for instance, child protective services, the juvenile court center, special education, or the mental health system. I found that the coordination of services often presents one of the biggest challenges and also can be one of the biggest benefits for a child.

I believe in giving every child a chance. We have to keep trying. The discouraging part is not so often with the child or the family because usually you can find something to work with, but it's often with the systems that the child and the family deal with. I think usually the system—or the people representing the systems—can work things out as they talk to each other. It's when they begin to act independently from their own perspective that I think clients get caught in the crunch. This week, we held a staff meeting because one agency had taken independent action for a child. They were perfectly justified from their perspective, but they didn't talk with the rest of us that had treatment plans in motion for the child. As a result, the child was uprooted from his placement and put in another place, and now his return to home is farther down the path then it used to be. That is probably because things weren't coordinated well.

One case illustrates the value of coordination. This little boy was about 9 or 10 years old and came to our attention on a referral from the School for the Blind and Deaf because he was "out of control." He was so out of control that his mom and his grandma couldn't handle him at home anymore. The school said they couldn't handle him. He didn't have language. He had about 30 words, and for a child his age, that isn't a whole lot. We had to hospitalize him because his behavior was so out of control. A lot of things happened, and the residential treatment center probably wasn't the best placement for him. He had stayed there way too long, and they didn't seem to be able to control him. There were things that they did with him that weren't working. We tried to refer him to different residential treatment centers, hoping that someone would be able to pull together the educational treatment that he needed, but they all turned him down.

After being turned down by three residential treatment centers, we got creative in the staff meeting, and we built a program for this kid. We had the school, the regional behavioral health authority, and several other people who were involved with this kid in the staff meeting, and we created a wrap-around, intensive, in-home program for this kid. We taught mom and grandma more about how to handle him. We worked intensively with him and the schools, transported him back and forth, and got him medicated properly. The school started to see successes in him, and he started to be OK at home. He was manageable, and furthermore, he was now learning. He was learning signs. He wasn't dumb like everyone thought he was. When people started to pay attention and to work with him, he started to respond.

That is a success story, and it took the cooperation of all those people coming together and saying, "OK, let's try it," everyone chipping in a little bit. That is the beauty of what I have found in the work that I've done over the last 10 or 12 years in coordination for the kids. When you get people down to the table and get them thinking about a child and what they can do, they come up with the solutions.

❖ MICHAEL HUTCHINS

When Michael Hutchins comes into your life, he doesn't stop. He doesn't cut off his sexuality. He doesn't cut off his spirituality. He doesn't cut off his physical being. So when I come in, you are getting all of that. Now, it may be expressed and manifested in different ways, but I hope there is no place where it is not coming through. I hope that the people who encounter me experience that passion and that they experience that commitment to living life and making life a better place. My life is different because you are in my life right now. If you weren't here, my life would not be as it is right now. So all of us make a difference. Our decision is, "What kind of difference do we wish to make?" Are we living our lives in a congruent manner so that we can make a difference?

I guess part of my interest in social change came from growing up in a very political family as a kid. My parents were children of the depression. They had to work hard growing up to even survive. My mom and dad would tell me that there were times when they didn't know where their next meal was going to come from or where they were going to live. I had this sense of injustice in the world and wanted to address some of those issues. I decided that I had to do something to make the world different. As a counselor, I got frustrated helping people adjust to what I saw as dysfunctional systems. I wanted to work with individuals, and I also wanted to change the society in which those individuals lived.

I was doing that as a straight, white, middle-class male until I met a man who changed my world dramatically. I was in New Mexico teaching, and I came out as a gay man, made some major life shifts, went through 3 years with my former wife and kids all in pretty intense therapy. After 3 years, I left New Mexico and decided that I was never going to be able to go back into the closet. I had gone through hell. I decided that I needed to take a stand and help other people who were struggling with sexual orientation—not just by doing private work but also by bringing about a change in the society in which we live.

I took a job with the Department of Juvenile Corrections for 5-and-a-half years, again working with adolescents, working with being clear about who you are, being very much aware that the system within which those kids had to work was not just. I went into private practice in 1987. My first contract was with the juvenile court, so I was working with the juvenile court families. I went through this struggle of whether to come out as a gay man when I had juvenile court contracts. I had some dissonance within myself because I wasn't living true to who I was. So I started advertising in the gay media as a gay counselor and approached people at the juvenile court to let them know, assuming that that would be the end of my juvenile court contracts. In fact, it brought me many more contracts because I started to get referrals from probation officers who had kids who were struggling with sexual identity issues.

I think that the piece that has the most meaning for me is the stuff on sexual orientation because it's so close to home. I know personally what it's like to live with the dissonance of behaving one way and knowing at another level that there is something very different. I know of leaders in the field of counseling, psychology, social work who are closeted gay and lesbian people. It is painful for me to see them go about their work and not be able to acknowledge who they are. I hope that by being an out gay professional, I make it a safer place for people who come out after me so the generations that come after me won't have to do the kind of hiding that I did as a young professional. Wherever I can, I invite people to address issues of sexual orientation. I prefer to call it "sexual identity development" because it's not just about being gay or lesbian; it's about being who we are as healthy professionals. It is amazing to me that therapists will do therapy and never ask questions about sexuality. I know many counselors, psychologists and social workers, who would never touch that when they see a client. So that is part of my commitment, to somehow or another make the world a safer place to be who we are, whatever that is.

For instance, I'm working with an 18-year-old straight kid right now who is less homophobic than most people. If I had identified myself as a gay man at first, he probably would not have come back. It wouldn't have been safe for him. I've been seeing him for about 3 months. About the 5th or 6th session, he said to me, "You're gay, aren't you?" I had not disclosed that to him. I said, "Yeah." He said, "Cool. Fine." Then, he acknowledged that he knew that from the first session but was afraid to bring it up. As a result of my letting him set the pace, he brought it up at a time when it was helpful for him. He is now safe to explore some of the sexual stuff that is going on with him. He is clearly heterosexual—there is no question about that—and he is sorting through appropriate relationship stuff for 18-year-olds. How I set it up for him to be OK is that sometime within the first session, when he started talking about relationships, I simply asked, "Are the relationships you are talking about with men or with women?" He just looked at me and said, "With women." I said, "OK. Fine." So I set it up right from the beginning that it's OK to talk about your issues around relationships regardless of gender. That tends to be my style. I don't think I've ever lost a client because of my sexual orientation. When I first started in my practice, I was afraid of losing clients because of my sexual orientation. Through my own therapy and my own clinical supervision, I worked through a bunch of that stuff.

I believe that we do not serve our clients or our society well when our political agendas become part of the therapy. So while I have a political agenda, I am never going to try to make my clients conform to what I believe. The language that I use with the kids is that if I were the architect of your life, your life would probably look different. But I'm not the architect, you are, so my role is to help you be clear about how you want to live your life. For me, that's part of social justice: being who are you and going where you want to take yourself. It goes back to the fact that we all make a difference. What kind of difference do you want to make? For me, that is where personal and political come together.

I've been doing some current work with African American professionals. They are aware that the world is very different for black gay men than it is for me as a white gay man. The struggle with homophobia in the black community and racism in the gay community play themselves out. I spent some time with a man who struggled with that, and he is an attractive, black, gay psychologist who would really like to come out and is absolutely terrified—a university faculty member afraid that if he comes out, he is going to lose his job. And he is at a university where that could, in fact, be reality based. He says that struggles around race and sexual orientation are significantly more difficult for black, gay professionals. I've just been reading *One More River to Cross*, and it's the struggle of being a gay black man and how there is no support in most communities for integrating those two things. The difficulty for me is, as a white middle-class male, how do I help my African American, Latino, Asian gay brothers and sisters come out and fully be what they are?

I like to believe that the world is a different place, that health professionals are a little bit different as a result of my teaching and counseling, and that I've made a difference in some people's lives. I have to believe that. I was speaking with a man in his late 60s who said that one of the things he has come to understand is that the seeds that he has sown will not bear fruit until after his death; he may never see the results of what he has been doing. I've been thinking a lot about what he said. So maybe I won't see the results of what I've done. But as long as we are moving in the right direction, there is hope.

❖ LISA BRASCH

I always knew I wanted to work with kids, but it might not have happened if it hadn't been for the accident. I have an undergraduate degree in elementary education. When I got out of college, there were really no jobs in education. There were no boomer kids yet, and schools were closing. So I took a 10-year detour in the business world. I had starting thinking that I wasn't doing what I really wanted to be doing, and then I had this life-changing experience. I was thrown off a horse and broke my leg really terribly and nearly lost it. I spent a year in rehabilitation and having surgeries, and at that point, I decided to chuck everything and start over. So at the age of 33, I went back to grad school. I went from making about $50,000 a year to making about $12,000 a year. I was working two jobs and going to school. I just decided to jump into it and do what I needed to do to get it done. That's how it happened. I wasn't unhappy, but I didn't like what I did. I didn't dislike it, but it didn't mean anything to me. And the world was changing, too—I mean, walking by homeless people and feeling the guilt. I need to be one of the people who does something, who doesn't just walk by.

One thing about me is that I would not be great working with adults. I really like working with kids. I have worked with some adults in family therapy, but it was always in a setting where the child was the point of entry into the family. I really have a harder time cutting slack for adults and not saying, "Get over it and move on. You're an adult." A kid has a different kind of brain, and they're not as developed yet, so I can really be a lot more forgiving, where with most adults, I don't have the patience.

I've worked with many kids, but there are a few who really come to mind. This first one was a delinquent kid. He had come out of the county youth jail, had been there on a 30-day temporary detention—for over a year. Then the charges were dropped, and he was never even convicted of anything.

He was a black kid from the projects, probably didn't know any white people in his life. I think I was the first white person he ever had any real contact with. He was only 15, and he seemed bigger. He was very street smart; he looked older and was very muscular. He was in a shelter; I was his counselor, and he didn't need "no fucking counselor." The first several times I met with him, I had to have the group home coordinator who was this 300-pound, 6'4" guy standing in between us, because this kid wanted me dead. He just wanted to kill me and hated to even be in a room with me.

I kept telling him, I don't care what we do in counseling, we can sit and play cards. Just show me you can have a relationship with somebody. You don't have to sit here and tell me your deep dark secrets; that's not what this is. If you want to talk, cool, but that's not what I'm doing. This went on for a couple of months, and one day, he got this idea that he wanted a Ouija board. I said OK, and I went out and spent $25 on this stupid Ouija board and brought it in. He was shocked. We played it for about 10 minutes and then he never looked at it again. But that was it. All of a sudden, he trusted me.

Another case was an 18-year-old girl. She was very different than a lot of the clients I had. She was in a group home and was about to go into independent living. She was very bright, and I'd been working with her for a long time. She had a really horrible history. I think her mother was a substance abuser. She was more of a neglect case than an abuse case, and she lived with her grandma. She started having behavioral problems, and her grandma couldn't cope with it. Basically, she had been hospitalized for over 10 years. It couldn't happen today, but they used to just warehouse kids in these mental hospitals when there was really nothing wrong with them. That's what happened to her; she was institutionalized from the time she was 6 until she was 17. She was in a psychiatric hospital, and from what I could see, there was not a lot wrong with her. Some transient depression, but she had no major mental disorder at all.

All of her abuse was from caretakers, from professionals. I used to go out to her group home and do counseling. One night—we'd been working together for several months at this point—she decided to tell me every single incident of abuse she had suffered from professionals. She talked for 6 hours. She went on to tell me this story about a DCFS worker. She was a 16-year-old flirtatious girl, and she used to flirt with the guy. He asked her out to dinner, and she thought it was cool, some older guy likes her, and she goes. He horribly, brutally raped her, but that wasn't the part that killed me. What got to me was, he played Russian roulette with her. Then he beat her on the head with a gun, and she had stitches in her head. I mean, he cracked her head open. Then, from that day forward, every time she was in a different placement, he would call her and say, "I know where you are," because he had access to the computers. And she was afraid that if she told, he'd come kill her. I think that was a perfectly reasonable assumption. I could not go after this guy because he would have probably killed her. There was no question in my mind that this had happened to her.

We go through this whole thing for 6 hours, and it's almost midnight. I took her out to eat because I couldn't just leave her like that. So we went out, hung out for an hour, and I took her home. On my way home, I had to stop at the grocery store for something—probably cat food—that couldn't wait 'til tomorrow. I had to go to the grocery store at 1 o'clock in the morning. I go to the grocery store, and somebody bangs me with a cart by accident, and I started to cry. And I'm not a crier. I started sobbing because somebody hit my cart. I go home, and now it's 2 o'clock in the morning, and I call my boss. I'm having this nervous breakdown. She was great and wonderful, but she didn't get it. She didn't get what I was feeling. She thought that I was feeling like the world is a bad, scary place, and everyone was evil. That wasn't it, but I couldn't get across to her what it was.

For the next 10 days—if this hadn't happened to me, I wouldn't believe somebody telling me this; but now there's all these books and things about it, but there weren't at the time—I had what is now called *compassion fatigue*. I was having flashbacks of something that hadn't happened to me. I was seeing the gun. I kept seeing her in the car with this perfect picture, like I was there with the gun, and I kept thinking, "What if it goes off this time?" There was this panic that it could still go off; she could still die. I know it makes no sense. I was having nightmares and panic attacks and flashbacks of things that hadn't happened to me. It was the most bizarre situation I've ever felt in my life. My boss was really great, and what finally got me through it was that she reminded me that this kid was a survivor, and she was basically OK. She has the strength to get through this, and she did. She was safe. Finally, after about 10 days or so, it went away.

Unfortunately, I think that there are a lot of unethical people in this field. Everyone thinks that we are here to save the world, but a lot of people are here to work out their own issues. I don't always agree that this is the place to do that, and I hope you've worked it out pretty good before you get here. There are some people who really have their own agendas, and I've learned there are unethical people at every level. It's really disturbing. People need to be conscious of that and vigilant about rooting them out.

Let me tell you one more story, and this will illustrate what I'm talking about. This is more about a staff member than a kid. In my last job, I had a lot of delinquent kids in a group home setting, mostly first offenders, some with serious histories. I had to hire somebody new, and I interviewed this woman who had this great resume. She had been working as a therapist in a prison. I couldn't have anyone squeamish. You know, these kids did some awful things, and you could not be squeamish. You had to hold them accountable, but you also had to be their counselor. I mean, we weren't the cops. She said to me in the interview, "I can find strengths in double murderers." I said, "You're hired." No one has ever lied to me more than this woman. She was the most unethical person. We had this really good kid. He had been through a lot, had done a lot, but he'd been really stable for several years. He was decompensating around her, and I couldn't figure it. He was fine with everybody else and he was this mess around her—sort of threatening, not outwardly, but he had this controlled rage, like he was going to kill her. I couldn't figure out what was going on, and we finally called in a consultant. She admitted that she was trying to make him decompensate so he would be locked up, which is where *she* believed he belonged. We fired her, but that's what I'm talking about.

Do you know the starfish story? There is this famous social work story. These starfish got beached, and this little girl was throwing them back one at a time. There were thousands of them, and somebody comes by and says, "You can't save them all. Why are you bothering?" And she says, "That one is saved. That one is saved." And that's what I was saying about before I was a social worker, about walking by the homeless. It's having the power to be able to change things, and that's why I don't find it depressing. At least, I am trying, and I am hopefully making a change. Even if I don't this time, I'm still trying, and I'm not just sitting cursing the dark.

Epilogue

I have just finished the final editing of the interviews that compose this book. Reviewing, critiquing, analyzing, and celebrating the lives of 34 social workers leaves me with a clear sense of what has been learned by me personally—a deep sense of respect for social workers and the work they do, individuals who have found their calling in life. Social workers who find meaning derived from the simple pleasure of helping another person, meaning from the relationships formed with others, meaning from pursuing justice in the world, meaning from doing work that is considered spiritual in nature.

Although I lecture about the knowledge and skill needed to perform professional social work in my classes, I now know that the work of many social workers transcends knowledge and skill. It is often carried out in the form of a calling, a calling that is different for each person but that carries meaning and purpose into the day-to-day activities of the social worker. It may be important to help people find that meaning so they can persist in the difficult job of doing social work, develop their true selves, or find a greater connection between their work and their existence in the world.

This calling does not lessen the need for a professional perspective about social work practice. Our ethical obligation involves knowing what is good practice, critiquing our decisions, and getting feedback on our work. Although much of what is emphasized in this book is about the elusive and special qualities that many social workers possess, I do not want to suggest that knowledge and skill are not critical ingredients in helping others. They are essential. When evidence-based practice and critical thinking are combined with the personal characteristics of "doing good," then social work is well positioned to make a difference in people's lives.

Many, or most, of the social workers in this book demonstrate altruistic values in their work. These altruistic tendencies may be what form a lot of the calling to social work. People with strong altruistic values do appear to have stronger commitments to the service of others[1]. They not only have altruistic actions but also altruistic intentions—they want to do good with no expectation of reward. Elizabeth Day spoke of how growing up in South Africa brought a profound sense of empathy toward blacks. Her statement, "people are hurting more than you can put words to," provides a glint of her underlying compassion. Her direct experience of the discrimination that existed in her childhood environment created a devotion to love and respect everyone. Many of the social workers in this book spoke of the genuine caring for the people they are trying to help. Their call to service reflects an ongoing commitment of compassion. I was struck by Levonne Gaddy's memory of placing a child in a foster home and then discovering the foster father was "treating her like a prostitute." Her compassion is penetrating when she admits, "my heart hurts today for that decision and what happened to that girl." As I listen to the stories the social workers told, I believe there are some common threads that guide them to harness these caring qualities and avoid being dispirited in their work.

Six themes are reflected in these life stories: (a) being connected to others, (b) seeing privilege and honor in helping others, (c) reflecting on the meaning of life, (d) having a helping and meaningful relationship with others, (e) being guided by moral principle, and (f) creating a caring community. In some manner, one or more of these themes were present and offered some guidance for pursuing greater purpose in being a social worker.

❖ BEING CONNECTED WITH OTHERS

Many professionals have jobs that separate them from others in the world: They work in isolated cubicles, are fixated on a computer screen, or are consumed with hard labor. In contrast, a social worker often feels a strong connection with the larger world. Being connected to other people often breeds a greater sense of connectedness. Doing social work is being part of a larger effort, working toward the greater good. Peering into another person's existence, their trials and tribulations, can lead to a broader perspective on life. Gail Gibbons talks about how her work with refugees adds a global perspective to her life. Through this work, she sees the "triumph of the human spirit." Michael Pesce concludes his interview by talking about the core of why he does social work. He thinks of his mother, who never had a consistent home, and then declares, "It's important to give. It's important to try and make things better for people." His sense of connection with others can easily be felt. Levonne Gaddy reached out to others to build an organization for multiracial support. In one of the largest cities, Los Angeles, she created a mechanism to connect people to each other.

Social work is often described as connecting private troubles with public issues. The social worker's training and perspective recognizes the individual but is forced to look beyond the individual and consider the larger societal issue. The family caring for an older adult needs help with coping as a family, but why does society not provide better resources to help such families? What can we do as neighbors and community members to help our aging members? Because social workers feel this sense of connectedness, they are quite adept at seeing people's strengths and identifying people as resources for each other and society at large. Philosophically, we can ask, "What resources can be brought to bear on the problem?" rather than, "How can I help this individual with his or her problem?" Different perspectives can emerge from a strong sense of connection. For example, where someone sees corruption, a social worker may see differences in values and opinions; where someone would like to condemn, a social worker would be more likely to educate; and where someone would fight, a social worker might mediate.

❖ SEEING PRIVILEGE AND HONOR IN HELPING OTHERS

As I listen to these life stories, I realize that doing this type of work is indeed a significant privilege. The care of an abused child, the last words of a dying AIDS patient, the joy of an adoption, the life decision of a teenager—these are profound events in people's lives, and social workers get the privilege of entering and participating in these private affairs. The social worker knows the life of the homeless person; he or she has experienced hundreds of homeless lives. The struggles, the barriers to happiness, are repeated in many people's life stories. It makes sense that they should derive some meaning out of this experience.

Melinda Oliver reflected on her role as a social worker after attending the funeral of one of her elderly clients. In spite of the difficulties in working with this irascible client, it became clear to her that she assisted this person in preserving her dignity, she helped her achieve her goal. She observed, "It struck home in my heart—this is the purpose of what I am doing. It is to give people a good life." In a similar manner, Michael Pesce reflects on the simple but meaningful experience of having a child say "thank you" when he was removed from an abusive home. Cathy Sammons talks about the importance of informing parents about their child's developmental disability and her desire to be the person to do this because she wanted it done in an appropriate, respectful, and sensitive manner. "I would look into the eyes of a parent and while I was telling them this terrible news and though my heart was heavy with sadness, *I* wanted to be the one to tell them."

Social workers who enjoy what they do see the honor and privilege in sharing such in-depth human experiences. A lot of our day-to-day lives exists at the mundane level. When we ask our friends, "What have you been doing?" a common response is "Nothing." The people social workers are helping are not doing "nothing." They are at the crossroads of life, searching for direction and meaning. What an honor to be able to assist them in their struggle, to talk with them in a time of need, to assist them in obtaining resources, to hold their hand as they lay dying, to share some of life's biggest moments. Certainly, this work is filled with lots of sadness. But sadness can bring illumination and purpose to life.

❖ REFLECTING ON THE MEANING OF LIFE

Examination of the meaning of life is something I have always been attuned to. Much of helping reflects a philosophical perspective on life.

When I was an undergraduate student, I took a philosophy class, and our major text for the course was a book, *The Vitality of Death*,[2] written by the professor. He was an existentialist who saw helping as a personal experience in confronting choices in life and changing one's perspective on life. Once you come to realize the mortality of life, you can begin to live life more fully—hence the vitality of death. Sartre's definition of *responsible* is to "be the author of one's life." Helping people to be authors and write their life stories means confronting most of the very basic questions in life. Social workers are immersed in work where questions about the meaning of life are brought to the surface. What does it mean to take full responsibility for one's life? Do I, the social worker, have the courage to master changes in the same manner I am encouraging in my clients? In some instances, the focus of working with clients is about helping them build character and accept the responsibility of adulthood. Danelle Joseph says it eloquently: "If everybody took personal responsibility, we wouldn't have any problems because we would all do what we needed to do to take care of ourselves."

As social workers are exposed to the struggles of clients attempting to act responsibly, they often reflect on the meaning of their own lives. In discussing therapy, Yalom[3] notes,

> As participant, one enters the life of the patient and is affected and sometimes changed by the encounter. In choosing to enter fully into each patient's life, I, the therapist, not only am exposed to the same existential issues as are my patients but must be prepared to examine them with the same rules of inquiry.

Basic philosophical questions, such as "Why do I live?" provide a sense of direction for more pragmatic questions, such as "How do I live?"

Philosophical reflections are evident in many of the social workers' life stories. Michael Pesce ponders the irony of an "us and them" mentality, recognizing that at any point in time he could end up to be just like his clients—homeless, drug dependent, or without needed resources. Joyce Morgan waxes philosophical as she describes her life story, "There for the grace of god go me. Why me and why not you?" "Do you control your destiny or does your destiny control you?" is a question she struggles with as she sees delinquents who have very little control over their lives.

Sofia Ahmad has had some trying experiences in the domestic violence field. You can sense her ongoing questions about life that are driven by her work: "So many men are abusive, how as a society can we stop it?" "Are we getting anywhere?" "I may make a difference in a person's life every day, but how many more are out there without getting this help?" Anita Royal works in the Public Fiduciary's office and often sees elderly parents who desperately need help but are so estranged from their children that the children cannot or will not aid their parents. She raises her voice and begins a passionate plea: "Is life so difficult that we can't bring aid to our loved ones in their time of need? I always tell my friends and everyone I know that you never, never, want to get that estranged from a family member. I don't care what has happened in the past. As you become adults, you begin to forgive your parents. You only get one set of parents. You don't ask for them, you get them."

Although not dealt with directly, much of the encounter between the social worker and the client reverts back to questions about the meaning of life. And even if clients are not consciously attempting to answer those questions, the work of the social worker often brings these questions to the forefront of their lives. There is much uncertainty in doing social work, uncertainty in the process of doing social work and uncertainty in the outcome of the work. In the face of uncertainty, large questions often loom to engage one's mind in thoughtful reflection. Such intense work with others often leads to fundamental questions about life: "What is important to me in my life?" "Am I achieving what I truly believe I want to do?" By asking such questions, social workers can get closer to living a more "authentic" life, putting the heart back into one's existence.

❖ HAVING A RELATIONSHIP WITH OTHERS

With delight and candor, many social workers told me about personal and intimate experiences they had with clients. This is indeed a factor that helps motivate many social workers in doing their work. Many would usher forth stories about how a client had been deeply touched and helped by them. For many social workers, the client-worker relationship enters a realm that is emotional, personal, and intimate. Being with a man when he first learns about the seriousness of his cancer, realizing together with a woman that her marriage is not working, listening to a client disclose a history of sexual abuse—these are intimate accounts that strengthen the relationship between client and social worker. So much of doing social work includes a relationship with another person that includes hearing about another person's secret—something never told before, listening to sad stories, hearing tales of misfortune.

Johna Reeves tells an amazing story about complexity and need in human relationships. The mother is a drug addict and prostitute. She has three boys, 7, 9, and 11 years old. The boys ask Johna to "go get our mom; we want to see our mom." Several times a year, Johna goes downtown and finds her and takes her to the emergency room or detox center to get cleaned up. When the mother is ready, she brings her to spend several hours with her three boys. She isn't trying to change the mother's behavior but says,

> I have three children asking me to find their mom so they can have some time with her. When their mom leaves again, I process with them and try to help them develop some ability to cope with their situation and go on.

Not focusing on the need to treat or cure the mother's lifelong addiction, Johna instead attempts to bring together a family who love each other but do not have an avenue to share that love.

Social workers are often attuned to the intricacies of human relationships: creating new avenues of trust among family members that have been hurt by each other from abuse, taking an angry husband and wife by the hands and joining them together to dissolve the anger, showing confidence in a homeless person who is making decisions about new directions in his life. Moving clients away from resistance and encouraging them to take action in the world often takes interpersonal skill as social workers attempt what is often seen as the impossible: changing dysfunctional patterns of behavior. Sometimes, the answer lies within the relationship itself. What can I do in my relationship with this client to show them that the way they are interacting with me is the way they are interacting with others?

A natural consequence of this relationship is to reflect on one's own life in contrast to others. Do I appreciate what I really have when so many others have less than I do? Have I, as a parent, put in as much parenting effort as I am suggesting to my client? Is my marriage any stronger than the one I am working so hard to help rebuild? Having a relationship with others in this manner can create a perspective about the world that helps bring awareness to our lives.

❖ BEING GUIDED BY MORAL PRINCIPLE

Many social workers discussed their commitment to a spiritual lifestyle and how social work was part of fulfilling their spiritual goals. My original title for this book was *Angels of Mercy*. I changed it because *A Call to Social Work* was more fitting. However, "angels of mercy" is an apt description of many of the social workers I interviewed who had a deeply spiritual side to them.

For many people, helping emerged as a process of returning something to others, a process of giving back. Often, they had received a gift of help and felt compelled to return it or had a negative or hurtful experience and wanted to protect others so they might not experience the same. A sense of giving back or guidance by moral principle is evident in many of the social workers' stories.

Chapter 7, *A Healing Journey*, chronicles many social workers who describe difficulties, pain, and suffering that they endured and how they turned those experiences into a desire to give back to others. Joyce Morgan left home at 13 years old and grew up in shelters, foster care families, and an orphanage. She now dedicates her life's work to similar children. Danelle Joseph says that bad things happen to people, and it is our job to turn it into something good. She described a personal journey of doing just that after her son died of sudden infant death syndrome. Kathy Lortie's story starts with a painful description of the death of her baby and the failure of a social worker to provide her with needed support and counsel. Her story ends with a description of a baby girl dying in her parents' arms, the family singing together to the baby and dressing her in new clothes in preparation for the funeral. As a pediatric social worker, she helps families prepare for and accept the death of their children in a respectful, loving, and humane way—an experience that she did not have. Pat Bethard talks about how her father died of alcoholism and how she herself is a recovering alcoholic. She recalls the notion that "the curse becomes the blessing" and describes herself as a "wounded healer." She works as a substance abuse outreach counselor in a public housing community.

Brehony reminds us that "it hurts to care, to open the heart to the pain of others. And yet, the removal of barriers between ourselves and others has a mysterious nurturing force as well."[4] A social work student working in a cancer support group asked me, "Is it OK for me to cry when I am with my clients?" I raised that question to the social work methods class I was teaching. It was clear that students had varying opinions and had been given different answers by supervisors. I have listened to professional social workers give different opinions about how appropriate this is. But the question itself reveals deep compassion and sensitivity to others. Compassion is a deeply felt relationship with another person, especially those that may need help. Tibetan Buddhists call this *tonglen*, the process of giving and receiving. The person experiences the energy that opens them to the truth of another person's pain and suffering. How many other professional workers experience this kind of challenge in their work? Sometimes, social workers are simply taken with the pain and suffering of their clients, by the urgent need for caring and kindness.

Such experiences often beckon spiritual connections for people.[5] The Dalai Lama says plainly, "My religion is kindness." The Hindu perspective is that "the god in me recognizes the god in you." In working with the dying people of Calcutta, Mother Teresa says she is "caring for my beloved Christ in his most distressing disguises." Spiritual connections need not be cloaked in religious themes; for many, it is passion for social justice. However we describe it, the spiritual dimension is an important one for social work and is being increasingly recognized as such.

❖ CREATING A CARING COMMUNITY

Robert Coles refers to the call of service as a witness to idealism. These social workers' life stories are an inspiring account of their actions to be responsible for this world. Indeed, in the words of Dorothy Day, an important historical figure to social work, "There is a call to us, a call of service—that we join with others to try to make things better in this world."[6] Day, like many of the social workers I interviewed, looked at her work in terms of its overall significance to the nation.

In her book, *Ordinary Grace,* Kathleen Brehony asks a thoughtful question: "Is it more reasonable to accept that evil is ordinary but goodness is not?"[7] Her point is simple: We are not used to seeing goodness—we are exposed to more negativity in the world that goodness. My hope is that we can spread the word of the social worker's acts of benevolence across society at large. Compassion and caring can be promoted by the social workers who have accepted this as an important value in pursuing their purpose in life. You have borne witness to many acts of goodness in these pages, and others in society would benefit from a similar reading. As goodness becomes more accepted and shared, we can forge a stronger, more caring community. The Lakota Sioux, Black Elk, points to the pathway of creating a caring community: "Like the grasses showing their tender faces to each other, thus should we do, for this was the wish of the Grandfathers of the World."[8]

An important experience for many social workers is a sense of connectedness to the community, to the larger universe. Thich Nhat Hanh, the Vietnamese Buddhist, discusses the experience of being connected to the larger community that he calls *interbeing*: "When we see the nature of interbeing, barriers between ourselves and others are dissolved, and peace, love, and understanding are possible."[9]

Each social worker has become for me the "hero of an epic poem."[10] Listening to their stories, learning about their lives, I can now see the truly epic proportions of their calling. Their dedication, their contribution to the nation is, for me, heroic. Who will do the *social* work required to help individuals and families in need, organize communities for more humane living conditions, and correct some of the injustices in the world? It is the social workers. It is their call to social work that we can all be thankful for.

❖ NOTES

1. V. Jeffries, "Virtue and Altruistic Personality," *Sociological Perspectives* 41(1998): 151-166.
2. Peter Koestenbaum, *The Vitality of Death: Essays in Existential Psychology and Philosophy* (New York: Greenwood Publishing Group, 1971).
3. Irvin D. Yalom, *Love's Executioner* (New York: Harper Perennial, 1989), 13.

4. Kathleen Brehony, *Ordinary Grace* (New York, Riverhead Books, 1999), 202.
5. Brehony, *Ordinary Grace*. Material from the Dalai Lama, Hinduism, and Mother Teresa have been adapted from Brehony, p. 203.
6. Robert Coles, R. *The Call to Service: A Witness to Idealism* (Boston: Houghton Mifflin, 1993), 12.
7. Brehony, *Ordinary Grace*, p. 214.
8. Brehony, *Ordinary Grace*, p. 220.
9. Thich Nhat Hanh (1992). *The Art of Mindful Living*. A Sounds True Production audiotape.
10. Robert U. Akeret, *Tales From the Traveling Couch* (New York: W. W. Norton, 1995). The quote is attributed to Fromm.

About the Author

Craig Winston LeCroy, PhD, is Professor of Social Work at Arizona State University in the Tucson Component. He has been teaching social work practice for 15 years. He has published widely in the area of children's mental health, prevention, social skills training, adolescent treatment, and program evaluation, and is the author of six previous books.